Workshop on Scaling Up Multilingual Evaluation (SUMEval 2022)

Online
20 November 2022

ISBN: 978-1-7138-6318-2

Printed from e-media with permission by:

Curran Associates, Inc.
57 Morehouse Lane
Red Hook, NY 12571

Some format issues inherent in the e-media version may also appear in this print version.

Printed with permission by Curran Associates, Inc. (2023)

For permission requests, please contact the Association for Computational Linguistics at the address below.

Association for Computational Linguistics
209 N. Eighth Street
Stroudsburg, Pennsylvania 18360

Phone: 1-570-476-8006
Fax: 1-570-476-0860

acl@aclweb.org

Additional copies of this publication are available from:

Curran Associates, Inc.
57 Morehouse Lane
Red Hook, NY 12571 USA
Phone: 845-758-0400
Fax: 845-758-2633
Email: curran@proceedings.com
Web: www.proceedings.com

AACL 2022

SUMEval 2022
Scaling Up Multilingual Evaluation

Proceedings of the Workshop

November 20, 2022

Preface

Massively Multilingual Language Models (MMLMs) are trained on around 100 languages of the world, however, most existing multilingual NLP benchmarks provide evaluation data in only a handful of these languages. The languages present in evaluation benchmarks are usually high-resource and largely belong to the Indo-European language family. This makes current multilingual evaluation unreliable and does not provide a full picture of the performance of MMLMs across the linguistic landscape. Although efforts are being made to create benchmarks that cover a larger variety of tasks, languages, and language families, it is unlikely that we will be able to build benchmarks covering all languages and tasks. Due to this, there is recent interest in alternate strategies for evaluating MMLMs, including performance prediction and Machine Translation of test data. We believe that this is an important yet relatively unexplored area of research that has the potential to make language technologies accessible to all. The SUMEval workshop recieved submissions on techniques for scaling up multilingual evaluation. In addition, the workshop also included a shared task on performance prediction.

Organizing Committee

Kabir Ahuja, Microsoft

Antonios Anastasopoulos, George Mason University

Vishrav Chaudhary, Microsoft

Monojit Choudhury, Microsoft

Sandipan Dandapat, Microsoft

Graham Neubig, Carnegie Mellon University

Barun Patra, Microsoft

Sunayana Sitaram, Microsoft

Table of Contents

Conference Program

November 20, 2022

The SUMEval 2022 Shared Task on Performance Prediction of Multilingual Pre-trained Language Models

Kabir Ahuja[♠] **Antonios Anastasopoulos**[♦] **Barun Patra**[♠]
Graham Neubig[♥] **Monojit Choudhury**[♠] **Sandipan Dandapat**[♠]
Sunayana Sitaram[♠] **Vishrav Chaudhary**[♠]
[♠]Microsoft Corp.
[♦]George Mason University
[♥]Carnegie Mellon University

Abstract

The SUMEval Workshop's shared task involved predicting performance of multilingual PLMs across multiple languages when these models are fine-tuned with varying amounts of data in different languages. The training data was provided for performances of two multilingual models on four NLP tasks, and a baseline was shared with the participants to get started. For test data, the task had two variants for evaluation, *non-surprise* version where the performance was to be predicted for languages seen in the training data but with unseen configurations, and *surprise* version where the languages were unseen during the training. A total of five teams participated in the shared task with 15 submissions overall. The participants proposed addition of new features, feature engineering techniques and trained an ensemble of regression models for the task. The best performing team had an improvement of 64% in MAE over the shared baseline for the *non-surprise* variant, and a 17% improvement for the *surprise* variant.

1 Introduction

Multilingual Pre-trained Language Models (PLMs) (Devlin et al., 2019; Conneau et al., 2020; Xue et al., 2021; Patra et al., 2022) have been recently gaining prominence due their surprisingly effective cross-lingual transfer capabilities (Pires et al., 2019; Wu and Dredze, 2019). These models are pre-trained on hundreds of languages, and when fine-tuned for a task on a single language (pivot language), they can obtain reasonable performance on languages unseen during fine-tuning (but seen during pre-training). This zero-shot transfer capability while impressive has been found to be non-uniform across languages, and is especially worse on low resource languages or languages that are typologically distant from the pivot language (Wu and Dredze, 2020; Lauscher et al., 2020). Lauscher et al. (2020) showed that these limitations of zero-shot transfer can be addressed by collecting a small amount of data in different languages i.e. the few-shot setup that can substantially improve their performance.

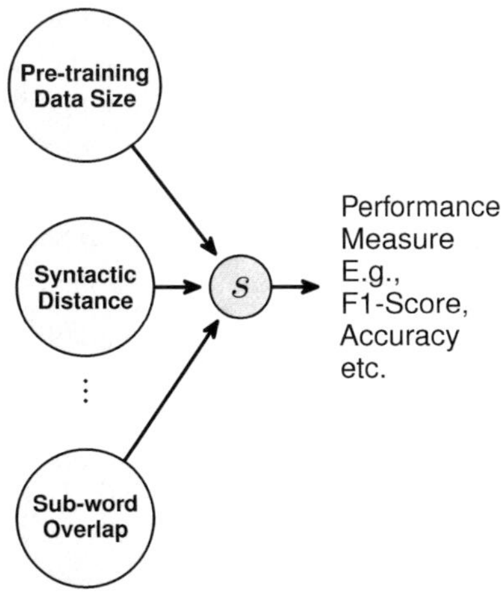

Figure 1: Performance prediction aims to learn a mapping between the factors influencing cross lingual performance of multilingual PLMs like Pre-training Data Size, Typological Relatedness

Despite the fact that these multilingual PLMs support hundreds of languages, most standard multilingual benchmarks (Conneau et al., 2018; Artetxe et al., 2020; Clark et al., 2020; Ponti et al., 2020) support evaluation for only a handful of these, and their performance on a large fraction of languages remain unknown. While creating standardised test sets in all of these supported languages will be an ideal solution, it can be prohibitively expensive to do so.

As pointed out in Ahuja et al. (2022a), performance prediction can be one possible remedy to this problem with multilingual benchmarks, by utilizing the linguistic and model-specific features influencing cross lingual performance to learn a mapping to the observed performance across different languages (See Figure 1). Utilizing regression models for predicting performance on NLP

Proceedings of the First Workshop on Scaling Up Multilingual Evaluation, pages 1–7
Nov 20–23, 2022.

tasks have been shown to yield meaningful estimates (Xia et al., 2020; Ye et al., 2021), and have also been shown to be effective at predicting performance of multilingual PLMs (Lauscher et al., 2020; Srinivasan et al., 2022; Ahuja et al., 2022b).

The shared task for Scaling Up Multilingual Evaluation (SUMEval) Workshop 2022 entailed this task of performance prediction, where the participants were given the performance of fine-tuned multilingual models XLM-Roberta (Conneau et al., 2020) and the Turing Universal Language Representation model (T-ULRv6) (Patra et al., 2022) for different training configurations across different languages and tasks to build their performance prediction systems. For evaluation there were two versions of the held out test sets, first a *non-surprise* variant where the participants were asked to predict the performance on languages for which some performance data was given in training but with unknown training configurations, and second a *surprise* variant where the performance was to be predicted on languages unseen in the training data.

Participants were provided LITMUS Predictor (Srinivasan et al., 2022) as a baseline to get started and were asked to build better systems possibly using additional features, and alternate prediction algorithms. We saw a participation of five teams for the task, with a total of 15 submissions. Different teams utilized new features in addition to those provided as part of the baseline, alternate feature engineering techniques, and utilized ensemble learning methods for building models. The best performing team on the *non-surprise* variant of the task obtained a 64% reduction in MAE over the baseline, and for *surprise* variant, the best performing team saw an improvement of 17%. To encourage further research in this area we have also made the baseline and datasets available publically[1].

2 Task and Dataset Description

We start by formally defining the performance prediction problem for the shared task. Consider a multilingual model $\mathcal{M}$ pre-trained on a set of $\mathcal{L}$ languages. $\mathcal{M}$ is then to be fine-tuned on some task $\mathfrak{T}$ with labelled data in $\mathcal{P}$ *pivot* languages, and then evaluated on a set of target languages $\mathcal{T}$, where both $\mathcal{P} \subset \mathcal{L}$ and $\mathcal{T} \subset \mathcal{L}$. A training configuration $\mathcal{S}$, is defined by the amount of labelled data for each pivot language $p \in \mathcal{P}$ used for fine-tuning $\mathcal{M}$. The fine-tuned model can then be evaluated on each of the target languages $t \in \mathcal{T}$ to obtain performance measure s, such that s is a function of:

$$s = f(t, \mathcal{S}, \mathcal{P}, \mathcal{M}, \mathfrak{T}) \quad (1)$$

In performance prediction, the objective is to learn this mapping f, given instances of input configurations $\{t_i, \mathcal{S}_i, \mathcal{P}_i, \mathcal{M}_i, \mathfrak{T}_i\}$ and output performance s_i, so that we can use this mapping to predict performance on unknown training configurations and languages. The input tuple $\{t_i, S_i, \mathcal{P}_i, \mathcal{M}_i, \mathfrak{T}_i\}$ is often represented using various linguistic, model, and data specific features. For a more detailed definition of the task and the features, we refer the readers to Xia et al. (2020); Ahuja et al. (2022a).

In the shared task, we provide the participants different training configurations and their corresponding performance on target languages for 4 multilingual tasks: i) XNLI (Conneau et al., 2018) for Natural Language Inference, ii) TyDiQA (Clark et al., 2020) for Machine Comprehension, iii) WikiANN (Pan et al., 2017) for Named Entity Recognition, and iv) UDPOS (Nivre et al., 2016) for Part Of Speech Tagging; and 2 mulitlingual PLMs: XLM-Roberta (large) and T-ULRv6 (large). The candidates were asked to build regression models using this performance data, and then were evaluated by testing on new training configurations and languages.

2.1 Dataset

The datasets were generated by fine-tuning the models across the 4 datasets along different training configurations and evaluating them on the target languages. The statistics of the datasets are given in Table 1. Training data was released to the participants in the beginning of the competition and the submissions were evaluated on the two variants of the held-out test data:

i) ***non-surprise***: In this test split the participants were asked to predict the performance on the languages for which there was some performance data available in the training set but the training configurations were new, i.e. for the different data allocations of the pivot languages.

ii) ***surprise***: In this test split the participants were asked to predict the performance on new languages, which were unseen in the training dataset (both as a pivot or target language). The training configurations were both new and the ones present in the

[1]https://github.com/microsoft/Litmus/tree/main/SumEval

Task $\mathfrak{T}$	Supp Models $\mathcal{M}$	Dataset Split	Number of Configurations S	$|\mathcal{P}|$	$|\mathcal{T}|$	$|\mathcal{P} \cap \mathcal{T}|$
XNLI	XLM-R and T-ULRv6	Train	40	15	15	15
		Test (*non-surprise*)	10	15	15	15
		Test (*surprise*)	50	15	10	0
TyDiQA-ID	XLM-R and T-ULRv6	Train	26	9	9	9
		Test (*non-surprise*)	3	9	9	9
TyDiQA-OOD	XLM-R and T-ULRv6	Train	26	9	11	3
		Test (*non-surprise*)	3	9	11	3
WikiANN	XLM-R	Train	400	39	39	39
		Test (*non-surprise*)	100	39	39	39
		Test (*surprise*)	500	39	17	0
UDPOS	XLM-R	Train	400	30	30	30
		Test (*non-surprise*)	100	30	30	30
		Test (*surprise*)	500	30	30	0

Table 1: Dataset statistics for the shared-task. Note that we have 2 versions of TyDiQA: TyDiQA-ID where both training and test set comes from the the original TyDiQA benchmark, and TyDiQA-OOD where the training data is from TyDiQA but test data is from XQUAD (Artetxe et al., 2020).

training data.

For validation, participants were provided scripts for performing Leave-One-Language-Out (LOLO) and Leave-One-Configuration-Out (LOCO) cross-validation from the training data, to help emulate the two test splits. In LOLO, one by one the performance data for each language is kept aside for validation and rest of the data is used for training the model. Similarly, in LOCO each unique configuration is set-aside one at a time for testing and remaining data is used for training.

3 Baseline and Submitted Systems

In this section we will describe the LITMUS predictor baseline and the top two submissions made for the shared task.

3.1 LITMUS Predictor Baseline

The LITMUS Predictor (Srinivasan et al., 2022) is an online open-source tool built to predict task-specific performance of multilingual PLMs across different languages and offering data-collection strategies to improve their performance. The tool utilizes the following features to represent the input tuple $\{t_i, S_i, \mathcal{P}_i, \mathcal{M}_i, \mathfrak{T}_i\}$:

1. Pre-training Data Size of t_i: Cross Lingual performance of multilingual PLMs have been observed to be dependant on the amount of data for a language that was present during pre-training (Hu et al., 2020; Lauscher et al., 2020), where the low resource languages for which the amount of data present in the pre-training corpora was low, are found to benifit less from cross lingual transfer compared to high resource languages. Hence, while predicting the performance for a language t_i we consider the $\log_{10}$ of the size (in tokens) of its pre-training corpus, given by $\texttt{PT-SIZE}(t_i) \in \mathbb{R}$

2. Amount of Fine-Tuning Data in $\mathcal{S}_i$: Fine-tuning multilingual PLMs even with small amounts of labelled data (few-shot-learning) has been found to drastically improve the performance in some cases (Lauscher et al., 2020). Hence, for the given training configuration $\mathcal{S}_i$ representing amount of fine-tuning data in each pivot language in $\mathcal{P}$, we use it as features for the predictor, given as $\texttt{FT-SIZE}(\mathcal{S}_i) \in \mathbb{R}^{|\mathcal{P}|}$.

3. Syntactic Distance between each $p \in \mathcal{P}_i$ and t_i: Target languages that are syntactically closer to the pivot languages have been observed to benefit greater from cross-lingual transfer than the ones that are syntactically distant (Pires et al., 2019; Lauscher et al., 2020). Hence, for predicting performance on t_i, we consider it's syntactic distance with each of the pivot languages $p \in \mathcal{P}_i$, which is computed using the syntactic features provided in the URIEL typological database (Littell et al., 2017). This is denoted as $\texttt{SYN}(\mathcal{P}_i, t_i) \in \mathbb{R}^{|\mathcal{P}|}$

4. Sub-word Overlap between each $p \in \mathcal{P}_i$ and t_i: Finally the sub-word vocabulary overlap between the two pivot and target languages that has also been shown to be important for cross lingual transfer (Wu and Dredze, 2019; Ahuja et al., 2022b) is also considered as a feature, denoted by $\texttt{SWO}(\mathcal{P}_i, t_i) \in \mathbb{R}^{|\mathcal{P}|}$.

These four family of features are then used to represent the input configuration which is used to estimate the performance value:

$$s_i \approx f(\texttt{PT-SIZE}(t_i), \texttt{FT-SIZE}(\mathcal{S}_i), \texttt{SYN}(\mathcal{P}_i, t_i), \texttt{SWO}(\mathcal{P}_i, t_i))$$

f can be approximated using any regression algorithm, and the LITMUS predictor by default uses XGBoost (Chen and Guestrin, 2016), and trains a separate predictor for each task $\mathfrak{T}$ and model $\mathcal{M}$ (which gives 8 predictors for our dataset).

3.2 PICT Team System

The team from Pune Insitute of Computer Technology (Patankar et al., 2022) made submissions for both *non-surprise* and *surprise* variants of the task. They proposed three feature engineering methods for the task in their submission: i) **Multi-Output** : The output of the regression model is expected to be a vector containing performance for each target language in the dataset, inputs are represented by the fine-tuning size of each pivot language; ii) **Single-Output** : Predicting performance of each target language separately, one-hot representations of the languages are appended to the input features; iii) **Single-Output w Language Features** : Apart from the pivot sizes, typological distance features (from URIEL (Littell et al., 2017)) between pivot and target pairs are also appended. The participants train a common model for all the four tasks and the two multilingual models by incorporating one-hot vectors for the two as input features, and encourage cross-task and cross-model transfer. For training the regression models they experiment with CatBoost (Prokhorenkova et al., 2018) and XGBoost.

3.3 GMU Team System

George Mason University team (Akter and Anastasopoulos, 2022) builds on the baseline system by proposing alternate feature engineering techniques and included additional input features for modelling the problem. The participants noted that the feature representation in the existing baseline system added a feature for each pivot language, which may not scale well when different combinations of the fine-tuning languages are used at the test time. They proposed a fixed-size featurization scheme which takes weighted sums of pivot-target overlap features, where the weights are decided by pivot sizes. Additionally, they propose two new features : i) **Presence of Target Language in Pre-training** : A binary feature indicating whether the target language was present during pre-training ; ii) **Target Language Writing Scripts** : A binary vector representing the writing script(s) of the target language obtained from van Esch et al. (2022). Additionally, the GMU team also trained models collectively for all the tasks and MMLMs, and used an ensemble of XGBoost, Multi-Layer Perceptron based regressors for their predictor model.

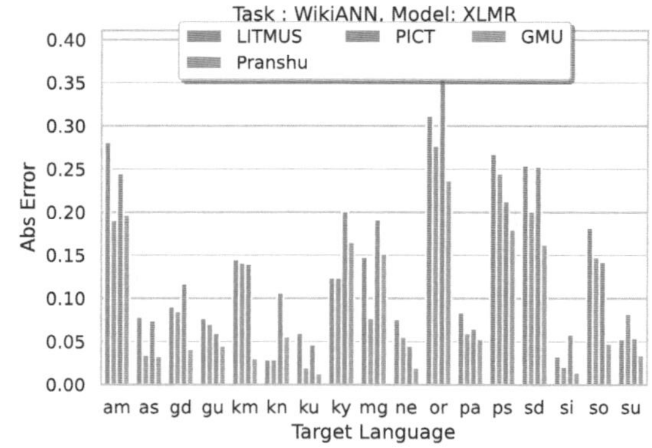

Figure 2: Language wise absolute errors on surprise languages for the baseline and the four submitted systems.

4 Results

We now compare the performance of the submissions and the baseline on both *non-surprise* and *surprise* test sets. Apart from `PICT` and `GMU`, we received submissions from three other teams that we identify by the usernames of the participants i.e. `Khooshrin`, `Viktoria`, and `Pranshu`.

4.1 *Non-Surprise* Test Set

The Mean Absolute Errors (MAE) on the *non-surprise* test set for the baseline and the submissions are given in Table 2. On average, all the submissions out-perform the baseline substantially, with `PICT` obtaining almost 64% reduction in the macro average error (91% in case of micro average). Analysing the task specific errors, we observe the maximum reduction in errors comes from the TyDiQA dataset. This might be attributed to the fact that out of the 4 multilingual tasks, we had the least amount of performance data for TyDiQA (26 training configurations as given in Table 1). Both `PICT` and `GMU` use joint training for multiple tasks which is in contrast to the baseline that trains individual predictors for each task (and model). Hence, the substantial drops in the errors are likely to be

System	Average Macro	Average Micro	TyDiQA TULRv6	TyDiQA XLMR	UDPOS XLMR	WikiANN XLMR	XNLI TULRv6	XNLI XLMR
LITMUS	0.018	0.131	0.351	0.381	0.005	0.017	0.026	**0.003**
Khooshrin	0.100	0.156	0.301	0.317	0.114	0.085	0.047	0.071
Viktoria	0.030	0.026	0.048	0.037	0.038	0.026	**0.004**	0.004
Pranshu	0.012	0.015	0.019	0.016	**0.006**	0.017	0.026	**0.003**
PICT	**0.011**	**0.011**	**0.012**	**0.014**	0.012	**0.011**	0.008	0.007
GMU	0.023	0.031	0.040	0.054	0.021	0.024	0.032	0.015

Table 2: Mean Absolute Errors (MAE) for the baseline and the submitted systems, on the *non-surprise* version of the test set.

System	Average Macro	Average Micro	UDPOS XLMR	WikiANN XLMR	XNLI TULRv6	XNLI XLMR
LITMUS	0.088	0.055	0.044	0.135	0.025	**0.017**
Khooshrin	0.118	0.070	0.152	0.099	0.016	0.015
Viktoria	0.097	0.064	0.067	0.131	0.028	0.029
Pranshu	0.075	**0.048**	**0.042**	0.109	**0.018**	0.022
PICT	0.104	0.070	0.071	0.141	0.032	0.037
GMU	**0.073**	0.052	0.062	**0.087**	0.026	0.035

Table 3: MAEs for the baseline and the submitted systems, on the *surprise* version of the test set.

attributed to multi-task training which is also in line with the observations in Ahuja et al. (2022b).

4.2 *Surprise* Test Set

Next, we compare the systems on the *surprise* languages test sets in Table 3. Here, teams GMU and Pranshu outperform the baseline with 17% and 14% reduction in macro average errors respectively. Maximum gains are observed for the WikiANN dataset, where GMU team obtains a 35% reduction in MAE. For UDPOS and XNLI tasks, GMU performs slightly worse compared the baseline, while Pranshu obtains comparable errors. We suspect this might be explained by oberving that the errors on WikiANN for the baseline are substantial ($\pm$0.135 points F1-Score) compared to the other two tasks, resulting in a better scope for improvement in the former dataset.

We also plot the (surprise) language specific errors on WikiANN dataset for the baseline and the four systems in Figure 2. As can be seen, GMU outperforms the other 4 systems for a majority of the languages, with less then 0.05 error in the F1-score for all languages except Amharic (am), Sindhi (sd), Kyrgyz (kr), Malagasy (mg), Oriya (or), and Pushto (ps) (6 out of 17 languages). This indicates that it might be possible to approximate the performance on new languages with a reasonable accuracy. However, there is still a scope of improvement as the worst case errors are still as high as 0.25 points F1-score for the best performing system.

5 Conclusion

In this paper we presented the findings from the SUMEval workshop shared task on performance prediction of multilingual PLMs. We received 15 submissions from five different teams, and most teams were able to obtain substantial gains over the baseline for the *non-surprise* test set, and two of the teams out-performed the baseline on the *surprise* test set with impressive gains. The strategy of training jointly on multiple tasks and models was utilized by multiple teams, and it lead to substantial improvements for low-resource tasks like TyDiQA. Additional features like the script of the target language were also found to be useful, specially for predicting performance of unseen languages. The best performing system achieved an error of less than 0.05 points F1-score for 11 out of 17 surprise languages for which no performance data was available for training. Overall, the results indicate a promising step towards scaling up the evaluation of multilingual models across multiple languages.

References

Kabir Ahuja, Sandipan Dandapat, Sunayana Sitaram, and Monojit Choudhury. 2022a. Beyond static models and test sets: Benchmarking the potential of pre-trained models across tasks and languages. In *Proceedings of NLP Power! The First Workshop on Efficient Benchmarking in NLP*, pages 64–74, Dublin, Ireland. Association for Computational Linguistics.

Kabir Ahuja, Shanu Kumar, Sandipan Dandapat, and Monojit Choudhury. 2022b. Multi task learning for zero shot performance prediction of multilingual models. In *Proceedings of the 60th Annual Meeting of the Association for Computational Linguistics (Volume 1: Long Papers)*, pages 5454–5467, Dublin, Ireland. Association for Computational Linguistics.

Syeda Sabrina Akter and Antonios Anastasopoulos. 2022. The GMU System Submission for the SumEval 2022 Shared Task. In *Proceedings of the First Workshop on Scaling Up Multilingual Evaluation*, Online. Association for Computational Linguistics.

Mikel Artetxe, Sebastian Ruder, and Dani Yogatama. 2020. On the cross-lingual transferability of monolingual representations. In *Proceedings of the 58th Annual Meeting of the Association for Computational Linguistics*, pages 4623–4637, Online. Association for Computational Linguistics.

Tianqi Chen and Carlos Guestrin. 2016. Xgboost: A scalable tree boosting system. In *Proceedings of the 22nd ACM SIGKDD International Conference on Knowledge Discovery and Data Mining*, KDD '16, page 785–794, New York, NY, USA. Association for Computing Machinery.

Jonathan H. Clark, Eunsol Choi, Michael Collins, Dan Garrette, Tom Kwiatkowski, Vitaly Nikolaev, and Jennimaria Palomaki. 2020. TyDi QA: A benchmark for information-seeking question answering in typologically diverse languages. *Transactions of the Association for Computational Linguistics*, 8:454–470.

Alexis Conneau, Kartikay Khandelwal, Naman Goyal, Vishrav Chaudhary, Guillaume Wenzek, Francisco Guzmán, Edouard Grave, Myle Ott, Luke Zettlemoyer, and Veselin Stoyanov. 2020. Unsupervised cross-lingual representation learning at scale. In *Proceedings of the 58th Annual Meeting of the Association for Computational Linguistics*, pages 8440–8451, Online. Association for Computational Linguistics.

Alexis Conneau, Ruty Rinott, Guillaume Lample, Adina Williams, Samuel Bowman, Holger Schwenk, and Veselin Stoyanov. 2018. XNLI: Evaluating cross-lingual sentence representations. In *Proceedings of the 2018 Conference on Empirical Methods in Natural Language Processing*, pages 2475–2485, Brussels, Belgium. Association for Computational Linguistics.

Jacob Devlin, Ming-Wei Chang, Kenton Lee, and Kristina Toutanova. 2019. BERT: Pre-training of deep bidirectional transformers for language understanding. In *Proceedings of the 2019 Conference of the North American Chapter of the Association for Computational Linguistics: Human Language Technologies, Volume 1 (Long and Short Papers)*, pages 4171–4186, Minneapolis, Minnesota. Association for Computational Linguistics.

Junjie Hu, Sebastian Ruder, Aditya Siddhant, Graham Neubig, Orhan Firat, and Melvin Johnson. 2020. Xtreme: A massively multilingual multi-task benchmark for evaluating cross-lingual generalization. *CoRR*, abs/2003.11080.

Anne Lauscher, Vinit Ravishankar, Ivan Vulić, and Goran Glavaš. 2020. From zero to hero: On the limitations of zero-shot language transfer with multilingual Transformers. In *Proceedings of the 2020 Conference on Empirical Methods in Natural Language Processing (EMNLP)*, pages 4483–4499, Online. Association for Computational Linguistics.

Patrick Littell, David R. Mortensen, Ke Lin, Katherine Kairis, Carlisle Turner, and Lori Levin. 2017. URIEL and lang2vec: Representing languages as typological, geographical, and phylogenetic vectors. In *Proceedings of the 15th Conference of the European Chapter of the Association for Computational Linguistics: Volume 2, Short Papers*, pages 8–14, Valencia, Spain. Association for Computational Linguistics.

Joakim Nivre, Marie-Catherine de Marneffe, Filip Ginter, Yoav Goldberg, Jan Hajič, Christopher D. Manning, Ryan McDonald, Slav Petrov, Sampo Pyysalo, Natalia Silveira, Reut Tsarfaty, and Daniel Zeman. 2016. Universal Dependencies v1: A multilingual treebank collection. In *Proceedings of the Tenth International Conference on Language Resources and Evaluation (LREC'16)*, pages 1659–1666, Portorož, Slovenia. European Language Resources Association (ELRA).

Xiaoman Pan, Boliang Zhang, Jonathan May, Joel Nothman, Kevin Knight, and Heng Ji. 2017. Cross-lingual name tagging and linking for 282 languages. In *Proceedings of the 55th Annual Meeting of the Association for Computational Linguistics (Volume 1: Long Papers)*, pages 1946–1958, Vancouver, Canada. Association for Computational Linguistics.

Shantanu Patankar, Omkar Gokhale, Onkar Litake, Aditya Mandke, and Dipali Kadam. 2022. To Train or Not to Train: Predicting the Performance of Massively Multilingual Models. In *Proceedings of the First Workshop on Scaling Up Multilingual Evaluation*, Online. Association for Computational Linguistics.

Barun Patra, Saksham Singhal, Shaohan Huang, Zewen Chi, Li Dong, Furu Wei, Vishrav Chaudhary, and Xia Song. 2022. Beyond english-centric bitexts for better multilingual language representation learning.

Telmo Pires, Eva Schlinger, and Dan Garrette. 2019. How multilingual is multilingual BERT? In *Proceedings of the 57th Annual Meeting of the Association for Computational Linguistics*, pages 4996–5001, Florence, Italy. Association for Computational Linguistics.

Edoardo Maria Ponti, Goran Glavaš, Olga Majewska, Qianchu Liu, Ivan Vulić, and Anna Korhonen. 2020. XCOPA: A multilingual dataset for causal commonsense reasoning. In *Proceedings of the 2020 Conference on Empirical Methods in Natural Language Processing (EMNLP)*, pages 2362–2376, Online. Association for Computational Linguistics.

Liudmila Prokhorenkova, Gleb Gusev, Aleksandr Vorobev, Anna Veronika Dorogush, and Andrey Gulin. 2018. Catboost: unbiased boosting with categorical features. In *Advances in Neural Information Processing Systems*, volume 31. Curran Associates, Inc.

Anirudh Srinivasan, Gauri Kholkar, Rahul Kejriwal, Tanuja Ganu, Sandipan Dandapat, Sunayana Sitaram, Balakrishnan Santhanam, Somak Aditya, Kalika Bali, and Monojit Choudhury. 2022. Litmus predictor: An ai assistant for building reliable, high-performing and fair multilingual nlp systems. *Proceedings of the AAAI Conference on Artificial Intelligence*, 36(11):13227–13229.

Daan van Esch, Tamar Lucassen, Sebastian Ruder, Isaac Caswell, and Clara Rivera. 2022. Writing system and speaker metadata for 2,800+ language varieties. In *Proceedings of the Thirteenth Language Resources and Evaluation Conference*, pages 5035–5046, Marseille, France. European Language Resources Association.

Shijie Wu and Mark Dredze. 2019. Beto, bentz, becas: The surprising cross-lingual effectiveness of BERT. In *Proceedings of the 2019 Conference on Empirical Methods in Natural Language Processing and the 9th International Joint Conference on Natural Language Processing (EMNLP-IJCNLP)*, pages 833–844, Hong Kong, China. Association for Computational Linguistics.

Shijie Wu and Mark Dredze. 2020. Are all languages created equal in multilingual BERT? In *Proceedings of the 5th Workshop on Representation Learning for NLP*, pages 120–130, Online. Association for Computational Linguistics.

Mengzhou Xia, Antonios Anastasopoulos, Ruochen Xu, Yiming Yang, and Graham Neubig. 2020. Predicting performance for natural language processing tasks. In *Proceedings of the 58th Annual Meeting of the Association for Computational Linguistics*, pages 8625–8646, Online. Association for Computational Linguistics.

Linting Xue, Noah Constant, Adam Roberts, Mihir Kale, Rami Al-Rfou, Aditya Siddhant, Aditya Barua, and Colin Raffel. 2021. mT5: A massively multilingual pre-trained text-to-text transformer. In *Proceedings of the 2021 Conference of the North American Chapter of the Association for Computational Linguistics: Human Language Technologies*, pages 483–498, Online. Association for Computational Linguistics.

Chenchen Ye, Linhai Zhang, Yulan He, Deyu Zhou, and Jie Wu. 2021. Beyond text: Incorporating metadata and label structure for multi-label document classification using heterogeneous graphs. In *Proceedings of the 2021 Conference on Empirical Methods in Natural Language Processing*, pages 3162–3171, Online and Punta Cana, Dominican Republic. Association for Computational Linguistics.

To Train or Not to Train: Predicting the Performance of Massively Multilingual Language Models

Shantanu Patankar[1*], **Omkar Gokhale**[1*], **Onkar Litake**[2], **Aditya Mandke**[2], **Dipali Kadam**[1]
Pune Institute of Computer Technology, Pune, India[1]
University of California, San Diego[2]
shantanupatankar2001@gmail.com, omkargokhale2001@gmail.com, olitake@ucsd.edu, amandke@ucsd.edu, ddkadam@pict.edu

Abstract

Evaluating the performance of Massively Multilingual Language Models (MMLMs) is difficult due to the shortage of evaluation datasets in low-resource languages. Due to computational limitations evaluating MMLMs trained on all possible pivot configurations is not feasible. This paper describes our contribution to the SumEval 2022 shared task, which handles the crucial task of Performance prediction of MMLMs. We build upon Microsoft Research's Project LITMUS and devise a method to further improve predictions. We develop various machine-learning approaches which outperform the baseline score provided by LITMUS. Our system ranked first with an RMSE score of 0.017 for the non-surprise and 0.109 for the surprise dataset.

1 Introduction

Massively Multilingual Language Models (MMLMs) are models that are pre-trained on a large set of languages and can perform various tasks. For example, a Massively Multilingual Neural Machine Translation model (Arivazhagan et al., 2019) is a single model trained on 100+ languages with over 50 billion parameters. Such pre-trained models work very well for zero-shot transfer across languages. However, the performance of these models is not consistent for all languages. They depend on factors like the pivot languages used for fine-tuning and the number of data points used for training. It is not feasible to evaluate the performance of the MMLMs on all languages. This is because some target languages are low-resource and lack proper evaluation sets for testing the performance. It is also difficult to train and test the models on all combinations of tasks, pivot languages, and target languages. This paper aims to develop a system that will take parameters like the MMLM model, task name, pivot languages, and the number of data points used for fine-tuning to predict the model's performance for the task on a particular target language. We develop two different systems. The first is for models fine-tuned on specific pivot languages and then tested on the same target languages. The second system is for models fine-tuned on a set of pivot languages and tested on surprise languages that were not part of the aforementioned set of pivot languages.

2 Related Work

Previously researchers have explored predicting the performance of machine learning models from unlabeled data by utilizing underlying information about data distribution (Domhan et al., 2015) or by measuring (dis)agreements between multiple classifiers (Platanios et al., 2014).

As the NLP Models are getting computationally complex to train, researchers have been interested in predicting the performance of NLP models without actually training them. Xia et al. (2020) have used ten different language features to train a XGBoost regressor. They compare the model's performance with predictions made by human experts. Dolicki and Spanakis (2021) leverage various syntactic features to implement a zero-shot performance predictor. Ahuja et al. (2022) demonstrate a single-task and multi-task performance prediction and discuss the significance of various linguistic features. Srinivasan et al. (2022) have developed LITMUS, a tool for prediction and labeling plan generation. We use LITMUS as a baseline for evaluating the performance of our system. We build upon all these past works by utilizing the syntactic features and tree-based models that have produced good results in the past and implement them on different configurations of data.

3 Dataset Description

The dataset consists of performance measures of XMLR and TULRv6Large, which are finetuned on

*first author, equal contribution

Proceedings of the First Workshop on Scaling Up Multilingual Evaluation, pages 8–15

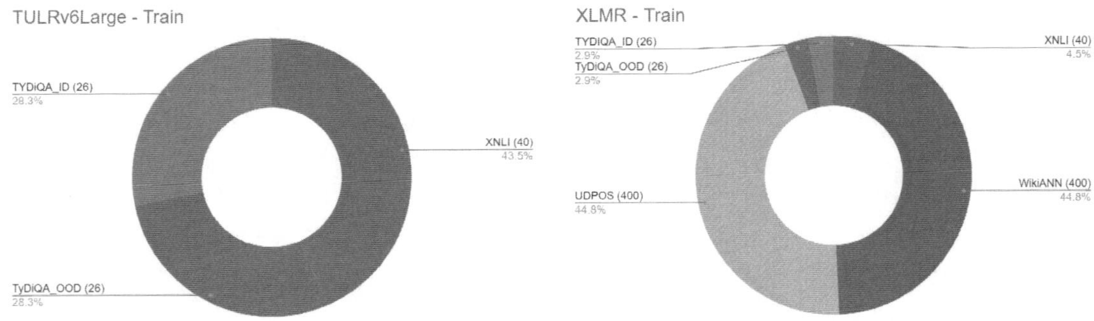

Figure 1: Data distribution of train data.

a specific set of languages (pivot languages) for four different tasks: XNLI (Conneau et al., 2018), WikiANN (Pan et al., 2017), UDPOS, and TyDIQA (Clark et al., 2020)). The dataset has 880 data points with distribution as shown in figure 1. Each data point has the model's training configuration, including the model name, task name, pivot languages, and evaluation results on specific target languages. The training configuration also contains the data used in each pivot language to finetune the MMLM. The evaluation results consist of the performance of the corresponding model on a set of languages. Instead of training a new regressor for every model-task pair, we observed that combining the data helps the prediction model gain better insights. Our four data combination techniques are described as follows:

- **Multi Output Dataset**: The total number of unique languages across all the individual datasets is 40. In order to combine the individual task-model pair-wise datasets, we create 40 columns each for training configuration and evaluation results (one column for each language). A zero in a pivot language column indicates the absence of that language while finetuning. We use this dataset to train a multi-output regressor.

- **Single Output Dataset**: We create a new row for each new evaluation language and provide the target language as an extra feature. We then use this dataset to train a single-output regressor.

- **Single Output Dataset with Language features**: We create an additional dataset by adding a few language features to it. We obtain the pair-wise genetic, syntactic, phonetic, geographic, inventory, and featural distances between target and pivot languages and utilize them as features for the model. These distances are calculated using the URIEL typological database. (Littell et al., 2017).

- **Surprise Dataset**: To predict the performance of MMLMs on surprise languages, we calculate the pair-wise syntactic, phonetic, featural, inventory, genetic, and geographic distances and the subword overlap between the target surprise language and the pivot languages. The target surprise language is also taken as a feature, but we encode the surprise languages with integers that are not present in label encodings of the pivot languages.

Model	Dataset Name	MAE	RMSE
XG-Boost	Multiouput	**0.007**	0.030
	Single output	0.015	0.052
	Single output feats	0.012	0.041
Cat-Boost	Multiouput	0.017	0.035
	Single output	0.012	0.034
	Single output feats	0.008	**0.017**
Litmus	Non-surprise	0.018	0.054

Table 1: Results for non-surprise data.

Model	Dataset Name	MAE	RMSE
XG-Boost	Surprise	0.093	0.128
Cat-Boost	Surprise	**0.082**	**0.109**
Litmus	Surprise	0.088	0.122

Table 2: Results for surprise data.

4 System Description

To get the relationship between different languages, we use different parameters used by Lin et al. (2019) like syntactic, phonetic, featural, inventory,

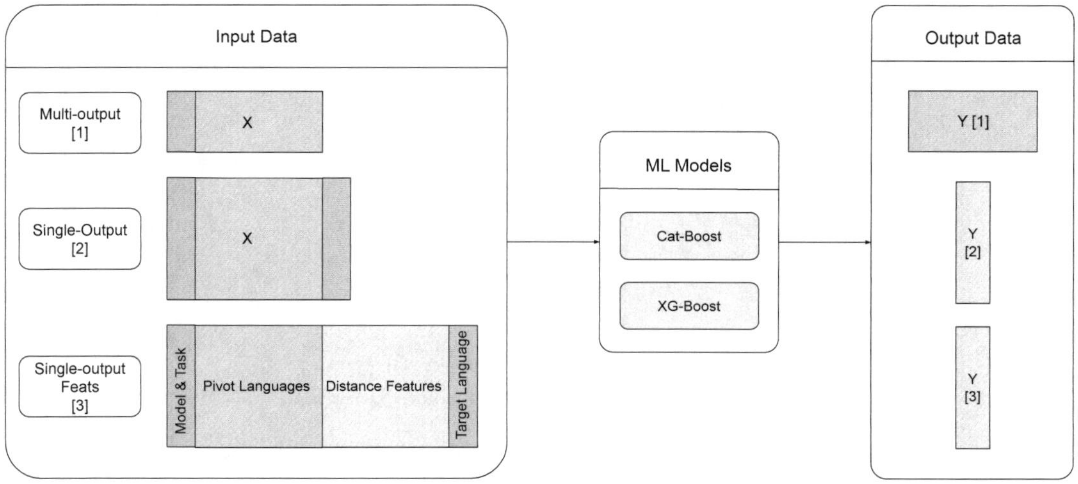

Figure 2: System Design.

genetic and geographic distances, and subword overlap.

- **Syntactic Distance:** The cosine distance between the feature vectors derived from the syntactic structures of the languages.
- **Genetic Distance:** The genealogical distance of the languages.
- **Geographic Distance:** The orthodromic distance between the languages, divided by the antipodal distance.
- **Inventory Distance:** The cosine distance between the phonological feature vectors derived from the PHOIBLE database.
- **Phonological Distance:** The cosine distance between the phonological feature vectors derived from the WALS and Ethnologue databases.
- **Featural Distance:** Cosine of all distances mentioned above.
- **Subword Overlap:** Percentage of common tokens in both languages

We have made two separate systems for performance prediction. The first one is for predicting the performance of the MMLMs on known languages, as shown in Figure 2. The second one is to for predicting the performance of the MMLM on surprise languages.

4.1 Non-Surprise system

We use the three datasets mentioned in section 3 to predict the performance metric of an MMLM on a target language.

4.1.1 Multi Output Model

The dataset has 42 features, 40 denoting the number of data points of the pivot languages, one feature for the model name, and one for the task name. Our targets are the evaluation scores of 40 target languages. We train different regression models like CatBoost (Prokhorenkova et al., 2018), XGBoost (Chen and Guestrin, 2016) and SVM as multi-target regression models on this data.

4.1.2 Single Output Model

The dataset has 43 features, 40 denoting the number of data points of the pivot languages, one feature for the model name, one for the task name, and one representing the target language. Our target is the evaluation score of an individual target language. This dataset is used to train XGBoost, CatBoost, and SVM regressors.

4.1.3 Single output with features model

The dataset has 283 features, 40 for the data size of each pivot language used for fine-tuning, and 240 are the pair-wise syntactic, phonetic, genetic, geographic, inventory, and featural distances of the target with the pivot language. The rest of the features are the model name, task name, and the name of the target language. We train the aforementioned three regressors on this dataset.

4.2 Surprise system

We use the Surprise dataset to train this system. As mentioned above in section 3, this dataset consists of the syntactic, phonetic, featural, inventory, genetic, and geographic distances and the subword overlap of the surprise languages with the pivot languages. The final training data consists of 563 features. 70 features are pivot languages, 490 are the 7 distance parameters of each of the 70 languages with the target surprise language, and the remaining three are for the model name, task name, and target language name. We train CatBoost with a maximum tree depth of 7 and a learning rate of 0.3. For XGBoost, we obtained the best results using the default parameters.

5 Experiments and Results

Our Training setup was pretty straightforward. Some of the observations we made during our extensive experimentation are as follows.

1. **Linguistic features improve the performance**:
   We observed that adding the seven linguistic features mentioned in section 4 improves the score of both the single output regressors. Adding pairwise linguistic features in multi-output data sets is not feasible as we need to add 11,200 new columns.

2. **Tree based models perform better**:
   We tried various regression models such as Logistic Regression, SVM, Multi-Layer Perceptron, Polynomial Regression, Lasso Regression, XGBoost, and CatBoost. We observe that XG-Boost and Cat-Boost are the top-performing models. We speculate this because tree-based machine learning models are good at handling complex, non-linear relationships.

3. **Target language: anonymous vs labeled**:
   When trained on a single output dataset, if we remove the labels of the target language, we observe a consistent but slight reduction in performance. This shows that the model makes informed choices based on the target language.

4. **Dataset: individual vs combined**:
   The model trained on the combined dataset produces better results than training individual models for Task-model pairs. This indicates that the insights gained by a model on a task are transferable.

5. **Features: PCA and Feature Elimination**:
   Performing Principal Component Analysis (PCA) on the extracted features reduces the performance of the models. This indicates that some important features are lost during the decomposition process. Feature elimination does not improve the model performance either.

6. **Eliminating individual language features**:
   We retrain each model by eliminating one syntactic feature and evaluate its performance. We find that eliminating any feature gives a lower overall score than we get by utilizing all the features. We also find that the importance of each feature from most important to least important is as follows:
   1. phonological distance
   2. inventory distance
   3. featural distance
   4. genetic distance
   5. syntactic distance
   6. geographic distance

6 Conclusion

In this paper, we have developed two approaches for the performance prediction of Massively Multilingual Models. One is for known languages, and another is for unknown or surprise languages. We have performed feature engineering on the data using different methods and tested different regression models on these features. For the non-surprise system, CatBoost gave the best performance on the single-output dataset with language features. On the surprise system, too, CatBoost outperformed all the other models. Both systems were able to outperform the LITMUS model. The system's performance can be further improved if more data is available for certain tasks like TyDiQA and XNLI.

References

Kabir Ahuja, Shanu Kumar, Sandipan Dandapat, and Monojit Choudhury. 2022. Multi task learning for zero shot performance prediction of multilingual models. *arXiv preprint arXiv:2205.06130*.

Naveen Arivazhagan, Ankur Bapna, Orhan Firat, Dmitry Lepikhin, Melvin Johnson, Maxim Krikun, Mia Xu Chen, Yuan Cao, George Foster, Colin Cherry, et al. 2019. Massively multilingual neural machine translation in the wild: Findings and challenges. *arXiv preprint arXiv:1907.05019*.

Tianqi Chen and Carlos Guestrin. 2016. Xgboost: A scalable tree boosting system. In *Proceedings of the 22nd acm sigkdd international conference on knowledge discovery and data mining*, pages 785–794.

Jonathan H Clark, Eunsol Choi, Michael Collins, Dan Garrette, Tom Kwiatkowski, Vitaly Nikolaev, and Jennimaria Palomaki. 2020. Tydi qa: A benchmark for information-seeking question answering in typologically diverse languages. *Transactions of the Association for Computational Linguistics*, 8:454–470.

Alexis Conneau, Guillaume Lample, Ruty Rinott, Adina Williams, Samuel R Bowman, Holger Schwenk, and Veselin Stoyanov. 2018. Xnli: Evaluating cross-lingual sentence representations. *arXiv preprint arXiv:1809.05053*.

Błażej Dolicki and Gerasimos Spanakis. 2021. Analysing the impact of linguistic features on cross-lingual transfer. *arXiv preprint arXiv:2105.05975*.

Tobias Domhan, Jost Tobias Springenberg, and Frank Hutter. 2015. Speeding up automatic hyperparameter optimization of deep neural networks by extrapolation of learning curves. In *Twenty-fourth international joint conference on artificial intelligence*.

Yu-Hsiang Lin, Chian-Yu Chen, Jean Lee, Zirui Li, Yuyan Zhang, Mengzhou Xia, Shruti Rijhwani, Junxian He, Zhisong Zhang, Xuezhe Ma, et al. 2019. Choosing transfer languages for cross-lingual learning. *arXiv preprint arXiv:1905.12688*.

Patrick Littell, David R. Mortensen, Ke Lin, Katherine Kairis, Carlisle Turner, and Lori Levin. 2017. Uriel and lang2vec: Representing languages as typological, geographical, and phylogenetic vectors. In *Proceedings of the 15th Conference of the European Chapter of the Association for Computational Linguistics: Volume 2, Short Papers*, pages 8–14. Association for Computational Linguistics.

Xiaoman Pan, Boliang Zhang, Jonathan May, Joel Nothman, Kevin Knight, and Heng Ji. 2017. Cross-lingual name tagging and linking for 282 languages. In *Proceedings of the 55th Annual Meeting of the Association for Computational Linguistics (Volume 1: Long Papers)*, pages 1946–1958.

Emmanouil Antonios Platanios, Avrim Blum, and Tom M Mitchell. 2014. Estimating accuracy from unlabeled data. In *UAI*, volume 14, page 10.

Liudmila Prokhorenkova, Gleb Gusev, Aleksandr Vorobev, Anna Veronika Dorogush, and Andrey Gulin. 2018. Catboost: unbiased boosting with categorical features. *Advances in neural information processing systems*, 31.

Anirudh Srinivasan, Gauri Kholkar, Rahul Kejriwal, Tanuja Ganu, Sandipan Dandapat, Sunayana Sitaram, Balakrishnan Santhanam, Somak Aditya, Kalika Bali, and Monojit Choudhury. 2022. Litmus predictor: An ai assistant for building reliable, high-performing and fair multilingual nlp systems. In *Thirty-sixth AAAI Conference on Artificial Intelligence. AAAI. System Demonstration*.

Mengzhou Xia, Antonios Anastasopoulos, Ruochen Xu, Yiming Yang, and Graham Neubig. 2020. Predicting performance for natural language processing tasks. *arXiv preprint arXiv:2005.00870*.

The GMU System Submission for the SUMEval 2022 Shared Task

Syeda Sabrina Akter and Antonios Anastasopoulos
Department of Computer Science, George Mason University
{sakter6,antonis}@gmu.edu

Abstract

This paper describes the submission of our multilingual NLP model performance evaluation system for the SUMEval 2022 shared task, a system for predict the performance of a model on a set of target languages. The system is based on the LITMUS model (Srinivasan et al., 2022), with the addition of 3 new features and model ensembling. Experimental results show that our system obtains a significant improvement than the baseline on both the test set and the surprised test set. Our system has achieved a 11% MAE reduction on the test set and is the best-performing submission on the surprise test set with 17% MAE reduction compared to the baseline.[1]

1 Introduction

Large multilingual models like mBERT (Devlin et al., 2019), TULRv6 (Microsoft, 2020) and XLM-R (Conneau et al., 2020) are becoming more popular as the foundation of NLP systems that can be used on more than 100 languages. However, most of the languages used in the evaluation of such massively multilingual models are still mostly high-resource ones. A large number of mid- to low-resource languages are not even used as part of the pre-training stage of dearth of unlabeled or labeled data. In addition, training and fine-tuning these large models to evaluate their performance for different combinations of tasks and languages is computationally very expensive. An alternate solution has been provided by making meta-models that can predict performance of multilingual NLP models without running the computationally expensive experiments.

Our submission for the SUMEval 2022 shared task focuses on improving the baseline performance of the LITMUS model by adding different features to the existing ones and using ensembling to improve the performance over the unlabeled test and surprise datasets. Our results show that our method is more effective than the baseline in predicting the performance in the evaluation for an existing as well as unseen set of languages for various settings. In fact, our system ensemble achieves the lowest error for the surprise language test set among the systems submitted to the shared task.

The organization of the rest of the paper is as follows. Section 2 presents the system description of our submitted predictor model. We present evaluation results and perform additional analyses on the SUMEval 2022 datasets in 3 and 4 respectively. We briefly discuss related works in Section 5, and Section 6 presents ideas for further expansion in future work.

2 System Description

Our system is built on top of the baseline LITMUS model (Srinivasan et al., 2022). We first describe briefly this baseline model (§2.1) and then discuss the additional features we use (§2.2). Our best submission consisted of an ensemble of models described in §2.3. From here on, we will be using the terms **target language** to indicate the language on which the fine-tuned model is evaluated (and whose performance we are trying to predict), and **pivot language** to indicate the language on which the model is fine-tuned.

2.1 The LITMUS Model

The LITMUS predictor is an AI assistant for predicting the performance of a multilingual language model like XLMR and mBERT on an NLP task without labeled test data and providing an estimated amount of labeled data needed to achieve the predicted performance for a set of known/unknown languages. The tasks that they focused on are XNLI (Conneau et al., 2018, natural language inference), UDPOS (Silveira et al., 2014, part-of-speech tagging) or WikiANN (Pan et al., 2017,

[1]Our code is available at https://github.com/syedasabrina/GMU_SumEval_litmus.git.

Proceedings of the First Workshop on Scaling Up Multilingual Evaluation, pages 16–20
Nov 20–23, 2022. ©2022 Association for Computational Linguistics

named entity recognition). The system introduces a set of factors that may influence zero-shot performance of a multilingual model. These features are largely based on the properties of the models:

Size of Pre-training-data is the $\log_{10}$ of the size of the pre-training corpus per language.

Typological Features capture the similarities based in hand-crafted features inspired by linguistic typology. The typological features for each languages are collected from the WALS database (Dryer and Haspelmath, 2013).

Type overlap with pivot language is a metric that signifies the overlap between the vocabulary of the target language and the vocabulary of the pivot language.

Distance from Pivot Language: is a metric signifying the distance between the target language and the pivot language. This metric is measured using `lang2vec` (Littell et al., 2017) that contains feature vectors for language features such as syntax phonology etc from WALS, SSWL and Ethnologue.

These features are used as an input to an `XGBoost` (Chen and Guestrin, 2016) regressor predictor model after converting them to a [0, 1] range using min-max normalization. The regressor is trained with a learning rate of 0.1, max depth of 10, squared error as the loss function and number estimators of 100 and the error is measured using Mean Absolute Error (MAE).

The evaluation is done under two settings based on the assumption of the availability of labeled test data for a particular target language. The labeled test data is considered unavailable by making the target language not appear in any of the training instances. The MAE of performance predictions across targets has been reported as 0.61%, 0.89% and 0.85% respectively for UDPOS, XNLI and WikiANN when the labeled test data is available and 8.08%, 4.62% and 9.93% when the labeled data is not available.

2.2 Added Features

We have added 3 new features to adapt the LITMUS model to our task-at-hand. Beyond the additional features, we also train the predictor across all tasks and models (as opposed to training a separate model for each task or MLM). The added features are described below:

Fine-tuning Feature: The baseline LITMUS model handles multi-pivot settings by adding $2p$ additional pivot features (capturing pivot-target overlap) for each of the p pivot languages present in the fine-tuning mix. However, under the shared task's settings, one could have different sizes on the combinations of fine-tuning languages with different data sizes used for finetuning. Hence, we decided to introduce a fixed-size "fine-tuning feature" to the LITMUS model, which is calculated using the following equation:

$$F = \overrightarrow{L} \cdot \overrightarrow{s}$$

where F = Fine-tuning mix feature, $\overrightarrow{L}$ = embedding created for each target language from WALS database (Dryer and Haspelmath, 2013) (similar to the ones already used by LITMUS) and $\overrightarrow{s}$ = data size for each target language to fine-tune the model. Essentially, we compute a single feature, which is the weighted average of the pivot-target overlaps, with the weights being proportional to the amount of data per language in the finetuning mix.

Presence of Target Language in Pre-training: This is a binary feature that indicates if the target language has previously been seen by the model in the pre-training phase.

Target Language Writing Scripts: According to previous works (Muller et al., 2020; Pfeiffer et al., 2020) pre-trained models have been shown to behave differently depending on the language's script. Hence, we have added the information about the writing scripts for the target languages as a feature. For all the languages that are being used in the systems, we have curated a list for all of their writing scripts based on information from van Esch et al. (2022). Note that for each script we have a binary feature depending on the script's usage from each language. Also note that some languages may use multiple scripts, e.g. Hindi both in Devanaghari script and romanized (using Latin script) were used in pre-training of XLM-R. Also note, though, that even though the resource of van Esch et al. (2022) may list multiple scripts for a language, it is not necessarily true that all such data are present in the pre-training or finetuning. We leave such changes to "cleanup" these features for future work.

Training the predictor across all tasks and models: The LITMUS baseline is trained separately for 4 different tasks (UDPOS, WikiANN, XNLI, QA) and for 2 different multilingual models (T-ULR and XLMR). For individual tasks, the predictor is trained on task specific datasets. We have trained the predictor on all datasets available for all tasks and models combined, using additional categorical features denoting the task and the MLM being modeled.

2.3 Ensemble Learning

Ensembling means combining the predictions from multiple regressors, which in principle should provide better predictive performance. For this task, we have combined the predictions of two different regressors (`XGBoost` and `MLPRegressor`) trained with the additional features on the combined models and combined tasks setting. Though it had a lesser impact on the test set, emsembling significantly improves accuracy on the surprise test set.

3 Evaluation Results

In this section, we are going to analyze the results of the experiments carried out for different test datasets. We have submitted 3 different systems for each test set and the performance is measured on Mean Absolute Error (MAE) and Root Mean Square Error (RMSE). They are the `all_tasks_combined` system, the `all_task_and_models_combined` system, and the ensemble system which are going to be referred as `GMU-Task`, `GMU-Task+Model`, and `GMU-Ensemble` from here onwards. The results for the test set and the surprised set for all 3 of these models are discussed in Sections 3.1 and 3.2 respectively.

3.1 Test Set Results

Based on official leaderboard results, the overall RMSE for the `GMU-Task`, the `GMU-Task+Model` and the `GMU-Ensemble` are 0.016, 0.016 and 0.023 and the MAE is 0.030, 0.030, 0.035. This indicates that the ensemble does not help much in improving the overall accuracy of the system. Training across all models (with the `GMU-Task+Model`) on top of across tasks does not improve over just training across tasks; this indicates that the performance of one model cannot be useful for explaining the performance of another model, at least not using the features we use.

Table 1 provides a breakdown of performance for the systems per task/dataset and language model. Based on the results we make the following observations:

- For UDPOS and WikiANN task, our `GMU-Task` model compares the most with the baseline model. The MAE and RMSE scores are on par between the two models.
- for the XNLI task, the baseline outperforms our best system `GMU-Task` by a large margin, a 78.57% MAE reduction for the XLMR model, and a smaller 13.33% MAE reduction for the T-ULR model over our system.
- For the QA task, our models significantly outperforms the baseline for both XLMR and T-ULR models. The `GMU-Ensemble` System has an 85.3% MAE improvement for the XLMR model over the baseline. Our `GMU-Task` System has a 93.62% of MAE improvement over the baseline for the T-ULR model.
- On average, our `GMU-Task` system has achieved a 76.47% MAE reduction for T-ULR model over the baseline while being on par with the average MAE of the baseline for the XLMR model. Hence, the `GMU-Task` system has an overall MAE reduction of 11% over baseline. Our improvement is attributed to the large improvement on the QA task.

Amongst all our submitted models, the `GMU-Task` system has the better performance numerically. However, `GMU-Task+Model` system is not very far off. These two models have very similar values of MAE and RMSE across tasks and models. The `GMU-Ensemble` has shown the best performance for the QA task for the XLMR but due to its comparatively poor performance over the other tasks, its average performance is poor amongst all systems.

3.2 Surprise Test Set Results

A surprise test set was available for the UDPOS, WikiANN, and XNLI tasks. Based on public leaderboard results, the overall RMSE for the `GMU-Task`, the `GMU-Task+Model` and the `GMU-Ensemble` are 0.10, 0.099 and 0.099, with the MAE at 0.080, 0.082, 0.073. This indicates that emsembling can raise the overall accuracy of the system on unseen languages and settings.

Table 2 presents a score breakdown as before. We summarize some interesting observations below:

- Similar to the test set, for the UDPOS task baseline outperforms our best system by 40.9% MAE reduction.

Model	UDPOS MAE	UDPOS RMSE	WikiANN MAE	WikiANN RMSE	XNLI MAE	XNLI RMSE	QA MAE	QA RMSE	Average MAE	Average RMSE
Baseline (as provided by the organizers)										
XLMR	**0.005**	**0.009**	**0.017**	**0.033**	**0.003**	**0.004**	0.375	0.376	**0.015**	0.043
T-ULR	-	-	-	-	**0.026**	**0.037**	0.345	0.349	0.119	0.194
Combining All Tasks: GMU-Task										
XLMR	0.009	0.014	0.019	0.034	0.014	0.029	0.104	0.130	**0.015**	**0.030**
T-ULR	-	-	-	-	0.030	0.040	**0.022**	**0.034**	**0.028**	**0.038**
Combining All Tasks+Models: GMU-Task+Model										
XLMR	0.009	0.013	0.020	0.035	0.017	0.032	0.081	0.098	0.016	0.029
T-ULR	-	-	-	-	0.030	0.041	0.037	0.051	0.032	0.044
Ensembling: GMU-Ensemble										
XLMR	0.021	0.032	0.024	0.037	0.015	0.021	**0.055**	**0.068**	0.023	0.035
T-ULR	-	-	-	-	0.032	0.042	0.042	0.050	0.034	0.045

Table 1: Results on the test data. Our models significantly outperform the baselines for the QA task (both models), and perform largely on par for almost all other tasks and models. We **highlight** the best performing model per task.

Model	UDPOS MAE	UDPOS RMSE	WikiANN MAE	WikiANN RMSE	XNLI MAE	XNLI RMSE	Average MAE	Average RMSE
Baseline (as provided by the organizers)								
XLMR	**0.044**	**0.059**	0.135	0.164	**0.017**	**0.020**	0.090	0.124
T-ULR	-	-	-	-	**0.026**	**0.028**	**0.025**	**0.027**
Combining All Tasks: GMU-Task								
XLMR	0.070	0.088	0.090	0.116	0.062	0.080	0.080	0.101
T-ULR	-	-	-	-	0.083	0.099	0.079	0.094
Combining All Tasks+Models: GMU-Task+Model								
XLMR	0.082	0.101	**0.080**	**0.099**	0.057	0.072	0.083	**0.100**
T-ULR	-	-	-	-	0.050	0.060	0.055	0.066
Emsembling: GMU-Ensemble								
XLMR	0.062	0.081	0.086	0.115	0.034	0.040	**0.074**	**0.100**
T-ULR	-	-	-	-	0.027	0.033	0.026	0.032

Table 2: Results on the Surprise Test dataset. The baseline model is the best for the UDPOS and XNLI tasks, while out GMU-Task+Model is the best for WikiANN. Note though that our GMU-Ensemble is the best *general* solution, performing the best across tasks on average.

- For the WikiANN task, our GMU-Task+Model has a 40.74% of MAE reduction over the baseline.
- The baseline has an improvement of 50% over our GMU-Ensemble for the XNLI task and XLMR model. However, for the T-ULR model, the performance are on par with each other.
- On average, the GMU-Ensemble has achieved an overall 17% MAE reduction over baseline making it the best general solution, performing the best across tasks on average. This improvement can be attributed to the average performance of the system being greater than the baseline for the XLMR model and being on the same level for the T-ULR model.

Amongst the three submitted systems, the GMU-Ensemble performs the best for the given dataset for the UDPOS and XNLI tasks for both XLMR and T-ULR model. However, the GMU-Task+Model outperforms the GMU-Ensemble for the WikiANN task. From the discussion above we can conclude that ensembling predictions technique can better the performance of the LITMUS model for the surprise test set.

4 Analysis

We have performed various analyses, choosing to focus on the surprise test set and the performance of our best-performing GMU-Ensemble model.

Task	Model	Config	Lang	MAE
UDPOS	XLMR	Diff	Galician	0.033
UDPOS	XLMR	**Same**	Galician	**0.026**
WikiANN	XLMR	Diff	Gujarati	0.027
WikiANN	XLMR	**Same**	Gujarati	**0.020**
XNLI	T-ULR	Diff	Bengali	0.017
XNLI	T-ULR	**Same**	Marathi	**0.016**
XNLI	XLMR	Diff	Panjabi	0.015
XNLI	XLMR	**Same**	Panjabi	**0.013**

Table 3: Lowest MAE's for languages across tasks. We can see for XLMR model, we get the lowest MAE's for the same languages across tasks regardless of configurations. Also, the same configuration data has better performance(highlighted) as the languages are seen by the models during pretraining.

Figure 1: MAE per task for surprise dataset. The `GMU-Ensemble` performs better overall. They have similar trend of values across tasks.

Semantic vs Syntactic Tasks According to the authors (Srinivasan et al., 2022), for the baseline LITMUS model, the predictor relies mostly on the pretraining data size feature for the semantic task and on the typological features and overlap between the language feature for the syntactic task. Figure 1 presents the MAE per task for the baseline and the `GMU-Ensemble` system. The baseline model has the best MAE score for the XNLI task, which is a semantic task and the other 2 tasks which are both syntactic tasks, has poor MAE compared to XNLI. The same trend of the MAE score is also followed by the `GMU-Ensemble` system attributing to the similar feature importance concept of the baseline model.

Performance per Language We also observe large variability in the performance of the `GMU-Ensemble` model across languages and datasets. Figure 2 presents a breakdown of the MAE on surprise tests per target language. The Oriya language has the highest MAE for the WikiANN task. Amongst all the tasks the XNLI task has the lowest MAE for the Panjabi language. The error ranges from 0.013 to 0.246.

Table 3 catalogs the languages with the lowest MAEs for each tasks and their configurations. Test configurations that are the same as the ones seen during training for each task almost always lead to lower MAE value than the test sets containing surprise languages as well as new configurations. The values reflect the common observation that the models will perform better if the target language has been seen by the model in the pre-training and/or finetuning step. his may also provide a supporting argument for works that promote an equitable allocation of data labeling across languages for multilingual models, e.g. Debnath et al. (2021). Also, it should be noted that regardless of the configuration, we obtain the lowest MAEs for the same languages per task (e.g. for UDPOS with XLMR the lowest MAE under both seen and unseen configurations is for Galician). The only exception is the combination of XNLI with the T-ULR model for Bengali and Marathi. For the XNLI T-ULR Same Configuration test set, we get 0.037 and 0.016 MAE scores and for the XNLI T-ULR Different Configuration test set we get 0.012 and 0.039 MAE scores for Bengali and Marathi respectively. The values are completely reverse of each other. This trend is consistent with other languages for these two datasets. The languages we get the lowest values for the XNLI T-ULR Same Configuration test set are the ones for which we get the highest values for the XNLI T-ULR Different Configuration test set, which is an interesting observation.

5 Related Work

Lin et al. (2019) first explored how to determine which high-resource transfer language can be used to maximize performance in a lower-resource target language in a traditional cross-lingual transfer learning scenario. Given the experimental settings as input, Xia et al. (2020) introduced the performance prediction task for simple cross-lingual transfer settings, constructing regression models that are similar to our system to predict the evaluation outcome of an NLP experiment. Experimenting on nine different NLP tasks, the study discovered that the predictors can make meaningful predictions over unknown languages and different modeling architectures, outperforming baselines and human expert predictions. Ye et al. (2021) then discussed how the task of estimating a system's performance without running the computationally

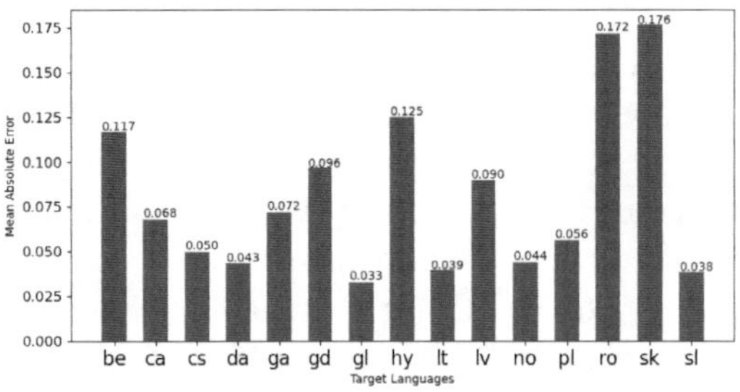

(a) UDPOS XLMR surprise langs diff config

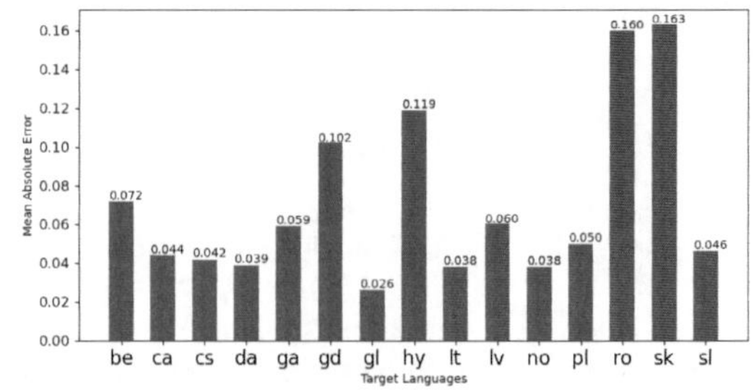

(b) UDPOS XLMR surprise langs same config

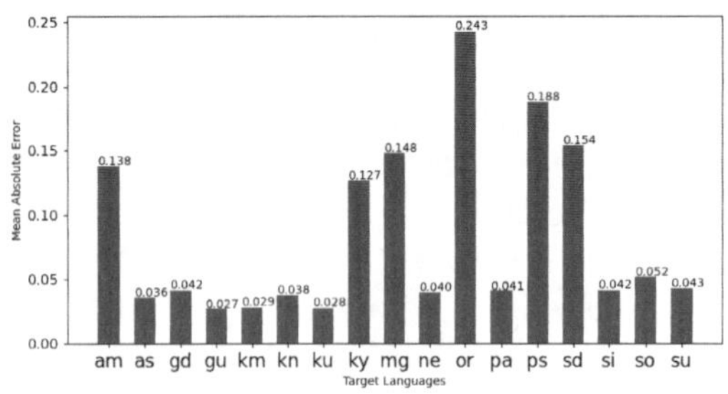

(c) WikiANN XLMR surprise langs diff config

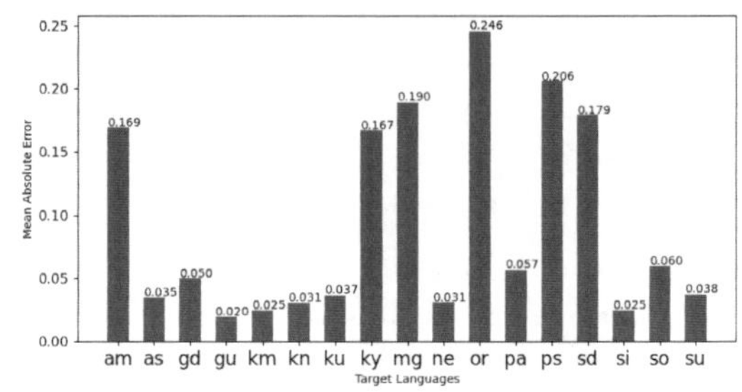

(d) WikiANN XLMR surprise langs same config

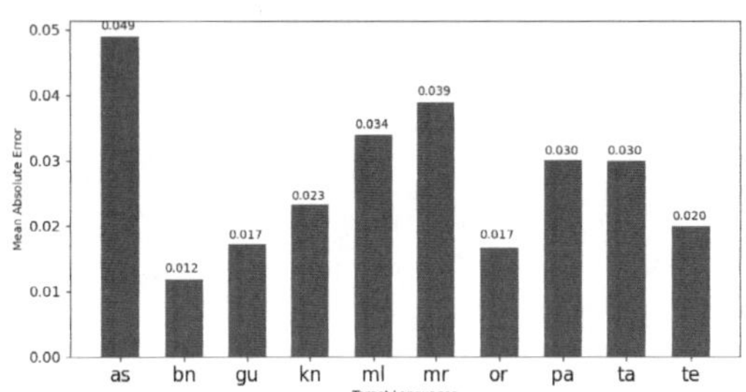

(e) XNLI TULRv6Large surprise langs diff config

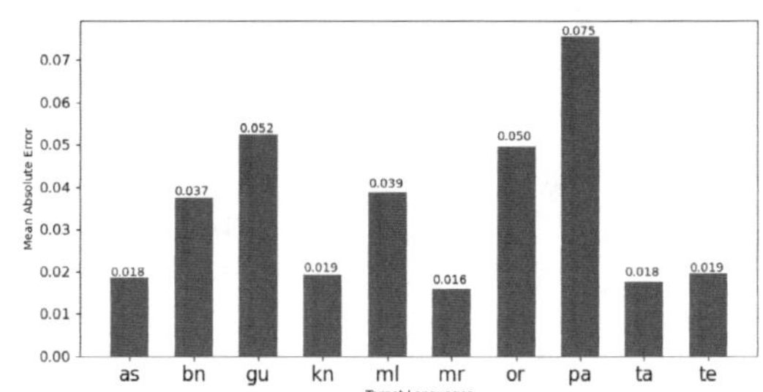

(f) XNLI TULRv6Large surprise langs same config

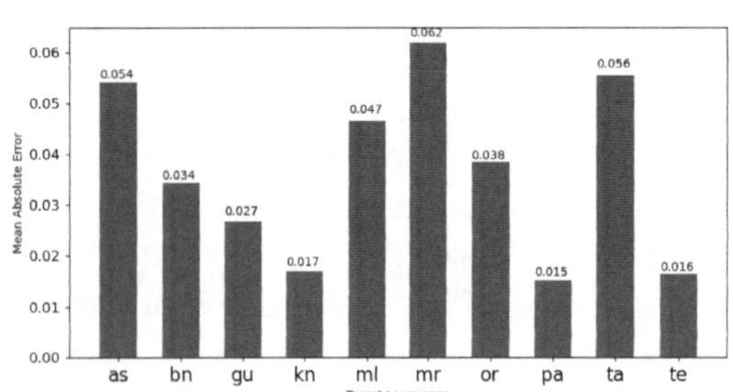

(g) XNLI XLMR surprise langs diff config

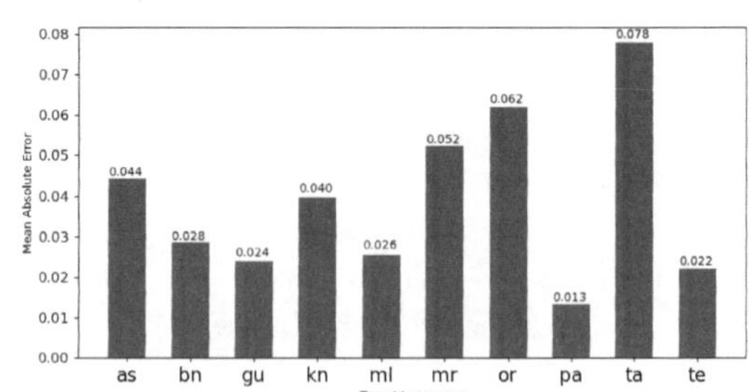

(h) XNLI XLMR surprise langs same config

Figure 2: Mean Absolute Errors for the surprise test set broken down by target language. Same languages have lower MAEs across tasks. The XNLI T-ULR dataset has the lowest MAEs for different Languages.

expensive experiments may aid in estimating performance of a language model for new datasets/languages. The study explores approaches for the reliability analysis of performance prediction models after examining the effectiveness of several such performance prediction models on four common NLP tasks.

6 Conclusion

In this paper we describe the GMU team submission for SUMEval 2022 shared task. Our system has extended the LITMUS model by including new features, combining data for training and using ensembling techniques that has improved the overall predictions for the test set.

Acknowledgements

This work was generously supported by NSF Awards FAI-2040926 and BCS-2109578.

References

Tianqi Chen and Carlos Guestrin. 2016. Xgboost: A scalable tree boosting system. In *Proceedings of the 22nd acm sigkdd international conference on knowledge discovery and data mining*, pages 785–794.

Alexis Conneau, Kartikay Khandelwal, Naman Goyal, Vishrav Chaudhary, Guillaume Wenzek, Francisco Guzmán, Edouard Grave, Myle Ott, Luke Zettlemoyer, and Veselin Stoyanov. 2020. Unsupervised cross-lingual representation learning at scale. In *Proceedings of the 58th Annual Meeting of the Association for Computational Linguistics*, pages 8440–8451, Online. Association for Computational Linguistics.

Alexis Conneau, Ruty Rinott, Guillaume Lample, Adina Williams, Samuel Bowman, Holger Schwenk, and Veselin Stoyanov. 2018. XNLI: Evaluating cross-lingual sentence representations. In *Proceedings of the 2018 Conference on Empirical Methods in Natural Language Processing*, pages 2475–2485, Brussels, Belgium. Association for Computational Linguistics.

Arnab Debnath, Navid Rajabi, Fardina Fathmiul Alam, and Antonios Anastasopoulos. 2021. Towards more equitable question answering systems: How much more data do you need? In *Proceedings of the 59th Annual Meeting of the Association for Computational Linguistics and the 11th International Joint Conference on Natural Language Processing (Volume 2: Short Papers)*, pages 621–629, Online. Association for Computational Linguistics.

Jacob Devlin, Ming-Wei Chang, Kenton Lee, and Kristina Toutanova. 2019. BERT: Pre-training of deep bidirectional transformers for language understanding. In *Proceedings of the 2019 Conference of the North American Chapter of the Association for Computational Linguistics: Human Language Technologies, Volume 1 (Long and Short Papers)*, pages 4171–4186, Minneapolis, Minnesota. Association for Computational Linguistics.

Matthew S. Dryer and Martin Haspelmath, editors. 2013. *WALS Online*. Max Planck Institute for Evolutionary Anthropology, Leipzig.

Yu-Hsiang Lin, Chian-Yu Chen, Jean Lee, Zirui Li, Yuyan Zhang, Mengzhou Xia, Shruti Rijhwani, Junxian He, Zhisong Zhang, Xuezhe Ma, et al. 2019. Choosing transfer languages for cross-lingual learning. *arXiv preprint arXiv:1905.12688*.

Patrick Littell, David R. Mortensen, Ke Lin, Katherine Kairis, Carlisle Turner, and Lori Levin. 2017. URIEL and lang2vec: Representing languages as typological, geographical, and phylogenetic vectors. In *Proceedings of the 15th Conference of the European Chapter of the Association for Computational Linguistics: Volume 2, Short Papers*, pages 8–14, Valencia, Spain. Association for Computational Linguistics.

Microsoft. 2020. Turing-nlg: A 17-billion-parameter language model by microsoft.

Benjamin Muller, Antonis Anastasopoulos, Benoît Sagot, and Djamé Seddah. 2020. When being unseen from mbert is just the beginning: Handling new languages with multilingual language models. *arXiv preprint arXiv:2010.12858*.

Xiaoman Pan, Boliang Zhang, Jonathan May, Joel Nothman, Kevin Knight, and Heng Ji. 2017. Cross-lingual name tagging and linking for 282 languages. In *Proceedings of the 55th Annual Meeting of the Association for Computational Linguistics (Volume 1: Long Papers)*, pages 1946–1958.

Jonas Pfeiffer, Ivan Vulić, Iryna Gurevych, and Sebastian Ruder. 2020. UNKs everywhere: Adapting multilingual language models to new scripts. *arXiv preprint arXiv:2012.15562*.

Natalia Silveira, Timothy Dozat, Marie-Catherine de Marneffe, Samuel Bowman, Miriam Connor, John Bauer, and Christopher D. Manning. 2014. A gold standard dependency corpus for English. In *Proceedings of the Ninth International Conference on Language Resources and Evaluation (LREC-2014)*.

Anirudh Srinivasan, Gauri Kholkar, Rahul Kejriwal, Tanuja Ganu, Sandipan Dandapat, Sunayana Sitaram, Balakrishnan Santhanam, Somak Aditya, Kalika Bali, and Monojit Choudhury. 2022. Litmus predictor: An ai assistant for building reliable, high-performing and fair multilingual nlp systems. In *Thirty-sixth AAAI Conference on Artificial Intelligence. AAAI. System Demonstration.*

Daan van Esch, Tamar Lucassen, Sebastian Ruder, Isaac Caswell, and Clara E Rivera. 2022. Writing system and speaker metadata for 2,800+ language varieties. In *Proceedings of LREC*.

Mengzhou Xia, Antonios Anastasopoulos, Ruochen Xu, Yiming Yang, and Graham Neubig. 2020. Predicting performance for natural language processing tasks. *arXiv preprint arXiv:2005.00870*.

Zihuiwen Ye, Pengfei Liu, Jinlan Fu, and Graham Neubig. 2021. Towards more fine-grained and reliable nlp performance prediction. *arXiv preprint arXiv:2102.05486*.

NTREX-128 – News Test References for MT Evaluation of 128 Languages

Christian Federmann and **Tom Kocmi** and **Ying Xin**
Microsoft
One Microsoft Way
Redmond, WA-98052, USA
{chrife,tomkocmi,yinxin}@microsoft.com

Abstract

We release NTREX-128, a data set for machine translation (MT) evaluation from English into a total of 128 target languages. The paper describes the data creation process and proposes a quality filtering method based on human evaluation. We show experimental results which confirm that the directionality of test sets translation indeed plays an important role wrt. the usefulness of the corresponding metrics' scores. Thus, we recommend that the NTREX-128 data set should be used for evaluation of English-sourced translation models but not in reverse direction. The test set release introduces another benchmark for the evaluation of massively multilingual machine translation research.

1 Introduction

Research on massively multilingual neural machine translation models requires test data to evaluate the models' quality. The creation of such resources is expensive—especially when one considers test sets for 100+ languages—so the amount of available test data is limited. This hinders progress.

While there already exist a few multilingual benchmark test sets more data will be needed to boost research efforts. Thus, we follow recent "open data" approaches undertaken in the field with this release.

As our research shifted its focus to massively multilingual models we started collecting test data for this scenario. We now release this data to the community as an additional benchmark for the evaluation of massively multilingual machine translation models.

NTREX-128, a data set containing "**N**ews **T**ext **R**eferences of **E**nglish into **X** Languages", expands multilingual testing for translation from English into 128 target languages. Our test data is based on WMT19 (Barrault et al., 2019) test data and compatible with SacreBLEU (Post, 2018).

We release NTREX-128 in the hope that it may be useful for the scientific community.

Data set	# of Languages
TICO-19	37
FLORES-101	101
FLORES-200	200

Table 1: Number of supported languages for three multilingual test data sets. Language sets do not fully overlap and text domains differ across the data sets.

2 Literature Review

Recently, the Conference on Machine Translation (WMT) has added a shared task on large-scale, multilingual machine translation. Such tasks require benchmark data sets for their evaluation. Three examples of such data are:

- TICO-19 (Anastasopoulos et al., 2020);
- FLORES-101 (Goyal et al., 2021; Guzmán et al., 2019); and
- FLORES-200 (#NLLB Team, 2022).

Table 1 shows the total number of languages supported by each of the aforementioned data sets. We will provide brief descriptions of all three data sets below.

TICO-19 is a data set released by the "Translation Initiative for Covid-19". It was a joint effort from several partners from academia and industry. The benchmark includes 30 documents (3,071 sentences, 69.7k words) translated from English into 37 target languages.

FLORES-101 is a data set released by Meta AI researchers. It includes 842 documents (3,001 sentences) translated from English into 101 target languages.

FLORES-200 extends the above data set to a total of 200 target languages. It is based on the same English source data as FLORES-101.

Proceedings of the First Workshop on Scaling Up Multilingual Evaluation, pages 21–30
Nov 20–23, 2022.

3 Data Set

3.1 Creation Process

To produce this data set we sent out the original English WMT19 (Barrault et al., 2019) test set ('newstest2019') to professional human translators. This work started after the release of the WMT19 test data and continued in parallel to our work on new translation models since then. Translators did have the full document context available but we do not know if (or to which degree) they have used this information.

3.2 Quality Assurance

Test data has to be of a high-enough quality level to be useful. We specified two main requirements: 1) we require translations which are performed by native speakers of the respective target language who are bilingual in English; and 2) reference translations should not be created based on post-editing MT output.

Our translation provider, as part of their translation process, performed quality assurance before delivery of the test set files. Upon receipt of the files we then sent them out to human evaluation via source-based direct assessment (src-DA), as implemented in the Appraise framework (Federmann, 2018). To avoid potential bias, annotation work was performed by an independent vendor.

As the result of the human evaluation process, we obtain segment-level quality scores based on the assessment of bilingual annotators who are native speakers of the respective target language. Scores range from $0 - 100$ and express the 'quality of the semantic transfer' between source and target language. This focuses more on adequacy than on fluency but, based on previous research findings, we consider this an acceptable trade-off.

Segments with scores < 25 are deemed defective, while any score in the $[25, 50)$ range is considered suspect. We return any segments with a score < 50 to the translation vendor for repairs. We have found that this method allows us to check quality for all translated segments; it scales well to thousands of segments with acceptable cost. As a side effect we have observed an increased level of quality control on the translation provider's side as they have understood that we will routinely verify their translation output for the full data sets, instead of random samples.

3.3 Avoiding post-edited reference output

Reference-based evaluation metrics, by design, have an inherent problem with reference bias. Even when dealing with professional translators there is a chance that reference translations may have been created by post-editing machine translation output. This is a problem for two reasons: First, it gives the respective MT system an unfair advantage in competitive evaluations. Second, it means that the reference translations are not independently produced anymore and, thus, may be of inferior quality compared to human translation from scratch.

4 Statistics

The NTREX-128 benchmark includes 123 documents (1,997 sentences, 42k words) translated from English into 128 target languages. More details are available in Appendix C.

5 Experiments

Based on the recent success of embedding-based, automatic evaluation metrics such as COMET (Rei et al., 2020), we run an experiment with the NTREX-128 data set in which we compare COMET-src scores for the authentic translation direction against the scores obtained in the reverse direction. As a secondary concern we investigate how COMET-src behaves for languages which it has not been trained on.

6 Results

We make the following observations:

- using COMET-src for quality estimation of test data is possible but limited as score ranges are non-comparable across language pairs;
- a sizable subset of languages sees COMET-src scores on translationese input scored higher than the corresponding authentic source data;
- while relative comparisons of COMET-src scores work for all language pairs there exists a subset of languages for which the scores appear broken. We suggest that this may be related to the fact COMET has never seen any training data examples for these languages.

See the `RESULTS` file in our repository for more details. As our main focus lies in the release of the NTREX-128 data set, we leave the further investigation of these points for future work.

7 Conclusion

We have presented our work on NTREX-128, a data set which contains 128 reference translations of the English 'newstest2019' test set originally released as part of WMT19. We intend to make it available as part of SacreBLEU. The test data will be released in the hope that it may be useful for the scientific community.

Acknowledgements

See the `CONTRIBUTORS` file in our repository. We would also like to thank the anonymous reviewers for their feedback.

References

Antonios Anastasopoulos, Alessandro Cattelan, Zi-Yi Dou, Marcello Federico, Christian Federmann, Dmitriy Genzel, Francisco Guzmán, Junjie Hu, Macduff Hughes, Philipp Koehn, Rosie Lazar, Will Lewis, Graham Neubig, Mengmeng Niu, Alp Öktem, Eric Paquin, Grace Tang, and Sylwia Tur. 2020. TICO-19: the Translation initiative for COvid-19. arXiv:2007.01788.

Loïc Barrault, Ondřej Bojar, Marta R. Costa-jussà, Christian Federmann, Mark Fishel, Yvette Graham, Barry Haddow, Matthias Huck, Philipp Koehn, Shervin Malmasi, Christof Monz, Mathias Müller, Santanu Pal, Matt Post, and Marcos Zampieri. 2019. Findings of the 2019 conference on machine translation (wmt19). In *Proceedings of the Fourth Conference on Machine Translation (Volume 2: Shared Task Papers, Day 1)*, pages 1–61, Florence, Italy. Association for Computational Linguistics.

Ondřej Bojar, Rajen Chatterjee, Christian Federmann, Yvette Graham, Barry Haddow, Shujian Huang, Matthias Huck, Philipp Koehn, Qun Liu, Varvara Logacheva, Christof Monz, Matteo Negri, Matt Post, Raphael Rubino, Lucia Specia, and Marco Turchi. 2017. Findings of the 2017 conference on machine translation (wmt17). In *Proceedings of the Second Conference on Machine Translation, Volume 2: Shared Task Papers*, pages 169–214, Copenhagen, Denmark. Association for Computational Linguistics.

Mauro Cettolo, Marcello Federico, Luisa Bentivogli, Jan Niehues, Sebastian Stüker, Katsuhito Sudoh, Koichiro Yoshino, and Christian Federmann. 2017. Overview of the IWSLT 2017 evaluation campaign. In *Proceedings of the 14th International Conference on Spoken Language Translation*, pages 2–14, Tokyo, Japan. International Workshop on Spoken Language Translation.

Christian Federmann. 2018. Appraise evaluation framework for machine translation. In *Proceedings of the 27th International Conference on Computational Linguistics: System Demonstrations*, pages 86–88, Santa Fe, New Mexico. Association for Computational Linguistics.

Naman Goyal, Cynthia Gao, Vishrav Chaudhary, Peng-Jen Chen, Guillaume Wenzek, Da Ju, Sanjana Krishnan, Marc'Aurelio Ranzato, Francisco Guzmán, and Angela Fan. 2021. The flores-101 evaluation benchmark for low-resource and multilingual machine translation.

Yvette Graham, Timothy Baldwin, Alistair Moffat, and Justin Zobel. 2013. Continuous measurement scales in human evaluation of machine translation. In *Proceedings of the 7th Linguistic Annotation Workshop and Interoperability with Discourse*, pages 33–41, Sofia, Bulgaria. Association for Computational Linguistics.

Francisco Guzmán, Peng-Jen Chen, Myle Ott, Juan Pino, Guillaume Lample, Philipp Koehn, Vishrav Chaudhary, and Marc'Aurelio Ranzato. 2019. Two new evaluation datasets for low-resource machine translation: Nepali-english and sinhala-english.

James Cross Onur Çelebi Maha Elbayad Kenneth Heafield Kevin Heffernan Elahe Kalbassi Janice Lam Daniel Licht Jean Maillard Anna Sun Skyler Wang Guillaume Wenzek Al Youngblood Bapi Akula Loic Barrault Gabriel Mejia Gonzalez Prangthip Hansanti John Hoffman Semarley Jarrett Kaushik Ram Sadagopan Dirk Rowe Shannon Spruit Chau Tran Pierre Andrews Necip Fazil Ayan Shruti Bhosale Sergey Edunov Angela Fan Cynthia Gao Vedanuj Goswami Francisco Guzmán Philipp Koehn Alexandre Mourachko Christophe Ropers Safiyyah Saleem Holger Schwenk Jeff Wang #NLLB Team, Marta R. Costa-jussà. 2022. No language left behind: Scaling human-centered machine translation.

Matt Post. 2018. A call for clarity in reporting BLEU scores. In *Proceedings of the Third Conference on Machine Translation: Research Papers*, pages 186–191, Belgium, Brussels. Association for Computational Linguistics.

Ricardo Rei, Craig Stewart, Ana C Farinha, and Alon Lavie. 2020. COMET: A neural framework for MT evaluation. In *Proceedings of the 2020 Conference on Empirical Methods in Natural Language Processing (EMNLP)*, pages 2685–2702, Online. Association for Computational Linguistics.

A License

See the `LICENSE` file in our repository. In addition to these license terms we ask that you cite this paper when using NTREX-128 in your work. Thank you.

B Download

NTREX-128 data is available from our GitHub repository: `https://github.com/MicrosoftTranslator/NTREX`.

C List of languages

The NTREX-128 data set covers the following set of 128 languages or language variants:

Afrikaans, Albanian, Amharic, Arabic, Azerbaijani, Bangla, Bashkir, Bosnian, Bulgarian, Burmese, Cantonese, Catalan, Central Kurdish, Chinese, Chuvash, Croatian, Czech, Danish, Dari, Divehi, Dutch, English, Estonian, Faroese, Fijian, Filipino, Finnish, French, Galician, Georgian, German, Greek, Gujarati, Haitian Creole, Hebrew, Hindi, Hmong, Hungarian, Icelandic, Indonesian, Inuinnaqtun, Inuktitut, Irish, isiZulu, Italian, Japanese, Kannada, Kazakh, Khmer, Kiswahili, Korean, Kurdish, Kyrgyz, Lao, Latvian, Lithuanian, Macedonian, Malagasy, Malay, Malayalam, Maltese, Māori, Marathi, Maya, Yucatán, Mongolian, Nepali, Norwegian, Odia, Otomi, Querétaro, Pashto, Persian, Polish, Portuguese, Punjabi, Romanian, Russian, Samoan, Serbian, Slovak, Slovenian, Somali, Spanish, Swedish, Tahitian, Tajik, Tajiki, Tamil, Tatar, Telugu, Thai, Tibetan, Tigrinya, Tongan, Turkish, Turkmen, Ukrainian, Upper Sorbian, Urdu, Uyghur, Uzbek, Vietnamese, Welsh.

Note that the total count of language names is less than 128 as there are some languages for which we support multiple scripts or variants. For detailed information on language codes, see the `LANGUAGES` file in our repository, which is the most up-to-date version of this list.

IndoRobusta: Towards Robustness Against Diverse Code-Mixed Indonesian Local Languages

Muhammad Farid Adilazuarda[1], **Samuel Cahyawijaya**[3], **Genta Indra Winata**[2], **Pascale Fung**[3], **Ayu Purwarianti**[1]
[1]Institut Teknologi Bandung [2]Bloomberg
[3]The Hong Kong University of Science and Technology
faridlazuarda@gmail.com

Abstract

Significant progress has been made on Indonesian NLP. Nevertheless, exploration of the code-mixing phenomenon in Indonesian is limited, despite many languages being frequently mixed with Indonesian in daily conversation. In this work, we explore code-mixing in Indonesian with four embedded languages, i.e., English, Sundanese, Javanese, and Malay; and introduce IndoRobusta[1], a framework to evaluate and improve the code-mixing robustness. Our analysis shows that the pre-training corpus bias affects the model's ability to better handle Indonesian-English code-mixing when compared to other local languages, despite having higher language diversity.

1 Introduction

Recent developments in Indonesian Natural Language Processing (NLP) have introduced an immense improvement in many aspects, including standardized benchmarks (Wilie et al., 2020; Cahyawijaya et al., 2021; Koto et al., 2020; Winata et al., 2022), large pre-trained language model (LM) (Wilie et al., 2020; Cahyawijaya et al., 2021; Koto et al., 2020), and resource expansion covering local Indonesian languages (Tri Apriani, 2016; Dewi et al., 2020; Khaikal and Suryani, 2021). Despite all these significant efforts, only a few studies focus on tackling the code-mixing phenomenon that naturally occurs in the Indonesian language. Code-mixing [2] is an interesting phenomenon where people change between languages and mix them in a conversation or sentence. In Indonesia, many people speak at least two languages (i.e., Indonesian and a local language) in their day-to-day conversation (Aji et al., 2022), and use diverse written and spoken styles specific to their home regions.

Inspired by the frequently occurring code-mixing phenomenon in Indonesian, we want to answer two research questions "*Is the LMs performance susceptible to linguistically diverse Indonesian code-mixed text?*" and "*How can we improve the model's robustness against a variety of mixed-language texts?*". Therefore, we introduce IndoRobusta, a framework to assess and improve code-mixed robustness. Using our IndoRobusta-Blend, we conduct experiments to evaluate existing pre-trained LMs using code-mixed language scenario to simulate the code-mixing phenomenon. We focus on Indonesian as the matrix language (L1) and the local language as the embedded language (L2) (Myers-Scotton and Jake, 2009).We measure the robustness of Indonesian code-mixed sentences for English (en) and three local languages, i.e, Sundanese (su), Javanese (jv), and Malay (ms)[3] on sentiment and emotion classification tasks. In addition, we explore methods to improve the robustness of LMs to code-mixed text. Using our IndoRobusta-Shot, we perform adversarial training to improve the code-mixed robustness of LMs. We explore three kinds of tuning strategies: 1) code-mix only, 2) two-steps, and 3) joint training, and empirically search for the best strategy to improve the model robustness on code-mixed data.

We summarize our contribution as follows:

- We develop a benchmark to assess the robustness of monolingual and multilingual LMs on four L2 code-mixed languages covering English (en), Sundanese (su), Javanese (jv), and Malay (ms);
- We introduce various adversarial tuning strategies to better improve the code-mixing robustness of LMs. Our best strategy improves the

[1]We will release the code upon acceptance. We provide the anonymized code repository at https://anonymous.4open.science/r/indorobusta-1403/

[2]In our case, code-mixing refers to intra-sentential code-switching where the language alternation occurs in the sentence.

[3]Malay is not a direct Indonesian local language, but it is considered as the parent language to many of Indonesian local languages such as Jambi, Malay, Minangkabau, and Betawi.

Proceedings of the First Workshop on Scaling Up Multilingual Evaluation, pages 31–34
Nov 20–23, 2022. ©2022 Association for Computational Linguistics

accuracy by ~5% on the code-mixed test set and ~2% on the monolingual test set;

- We show that existing LMs are more robust to English code-mixing rather than to local languages code-mixing and provide detailed analysis of this phenomenon.

2 IndoRobusta Framework

IndoRobusta is a code-mixing robustness framework consisting of two main modules: 1) `IndoRobusta-Blend`, which evaluates the code-mixing robustness of LMs through a code-mixing perturbation method, and 2) `IndoRobusta-Shot`, which improves the code-mixing robustness of LMs using a code-mixing adversarial training technique.

2.1 Notation

Given a monolingual language sentence $X = \{w_1, w_2, \ldots, w_M\}$, where w_i denotes a token in a sentence and M denotes the number of tokens in a sentence, we denote a monolingual language dataset $\mathcal{D} = \{(X_1, Y_1), (X_2, Y_2), \ldots, (X_N, Y_N)\}$, where (X_i, Y_i) denotes a sentence-label pair and N is the number of samples. Given a token w_i, a mask token w^{mask} and a sentence X, we define a sentence with masked w_i token as $X_{\setminus w_i} = \{w_1, w_2, \ldots, w_{i-1}, w^{mask}, w_{i+1}, \ldots, w_M\}$. We further define a code-mixing dataset $\mathcal{D}' = \{(X'_1, Y_1), (X'_2, Y_2), \ldots, (X'_N, Y_N)\}$ where X'_i denotes the code-mixed sentence. Lastly, we define the set of parameters of a language model as θ, the prediction label of a sentence X as $f_\theta(X)$, the prediction score of the label Y given a sentence X as $f_\theta(Y|X)$, and the prediction score of the label other than Y given a sentence X as $f_\theta(\bar{Y}|X)$.

2.2 IndoRobusta-Blend

`IndoRobusta-Blend` is a code-mixing robustness evaluation method that involves two steps: 1) code-mixed dataset generation and 2) model evaluation on the code-mixed dataset. The first step is synthetically generating the code-mixed example using the translation of important words in a sentence. To do so, we formally define the importance I_{w_i} of the word w_i for a given sample (X, Y) as:

$$I_{w_i} = \begin{cases} f_\theta(Y|X) - f_\theta(Y|X_{\setminus w_i}), \\ \quad \text{if} f_\theta(X) = f_\theta(X_{\setminus w_i}) = Y \\ [f_\theta(Y|X) - f_\theta(Y|X_{\setminus w_i})] + \\ \quad [f_\theta(\bar{Y}|X) - f_\theta(\bar{Y}|X_{\setminus w_i})], \text{otherwise.} \end{cases}$$

Algorithm 1 Code-mixed sample generation workflow in IndoRobusta framework

Require: Clean sentence example X, ground truth label Y, language model Θ, similarity threshold α, perturb ratio R, embedded Language L
Ensure: Adversarial Example X_{adv}
  $Y' \leftarrow$ PREDICT(Θ, X)
  if $Y' \neq Y$ **then**
    return X
  end if
  W $\leftarrow$R% highest I_{w_i} words in X
  $W^L \leftarrow$ TRANSLATE(W, target-language=L)
  $X_{adv} \leftarrow$ PERTURB(X, W^L)
  if SIM(X, X_{adv}) < α **then**
    while SIM(X, X_{adv}) < α **do**
      $W^L \leftarrow$ RESAMPLE(W^L, I_{w_i})
      $X_{adv} \leftarrow$ PERTURB(X, W^L)
    end while
  end if
  return X_{adv}

`IndoRobusta-Blend` takes $R\%$ words with the highest I_{w_i}, denoted as the **perturbation ratio**, and applies a word-level translation for each word. Using the translated words, `IndoRobusta-Blend` generates a code-mixed sentence by replacing the important words with their corresponding translation. To ensure generating a semantically-related code-mixed samples, we define a similarity threshold α to constraint the cosine distance between X and X_{adv}. When the distance between X and X_{adv} is below α, we resample the perturbed words and generate a more similar X_{adv}.

More formally, we define the code-mixing sample generation as a function $g(X, Y, \theta) = X_{adv}$. To generate the code-mixed dataset $\mathcal{D}'$ from the monolingual dataset $\mathcal{D}$ and a model θ, `IndoRobusta-Blend` applies $g(X_i, Y_i, \theta)$ to each sample (X_i, Y_i) in $\mathcal{D}$. Using $\mathcal{D}$ and $\mathcal{D}'$, `IndoRobusta-Blend` evaluates the robustness of the fine-tuned model θ', trained on $\mathcal{D}$, by evaluating θ on both $\mathcal{D}$ and $\mathcal{D}'$. More formally, we define the code-mixed sample generation in Algorithm 1.

2.3 IndoRobusta-Shot

`IndoRobusta-Shot` is a code-mixing adversarial defense method, which aims to improve the robustness of the model. `IndoRobusta-Shot` does so by fine-tuning the model on the generated code-mixed dataset $\mathcal{D}'$. Similar to `IndoRobusta-Blend`, our `IndoRobusta-`

Model	Orig.	en	jw	ms	su	avg
			EmoT			
IB$_B$	72.42	9.55	12.35	**9.47**	9.39	**10.19**
IB$_L$	75.53	**9.24**	**12.12**	10.23	**9.32**	10.23
mB$_B$	61.14	12.50	14.02	12.73	12.50	12.96
XR$_B$	72.88	10.98	13.94	13.18	12.50	12.65
XR$_L$	**78.26**	12.27	13.03	12.42	11.74	12.37
Avg		10.91	13.09	11.61	11.09	
			SmSA			
IB$_B$	91.00	**1.33**	5.07	3.20	2.40	3.00
IB$_L$	**94.20**	2.47	4.13	4.00	**2.20**	3.20
mB$_B$	83.00	2.20	**3.00**	2.93	2.47	**2.65**
XR$_B$	91.53	3.40	3.80	4.27	4.27	3.94
XR$_L$	94.07	2.13	3.20	**2.60**	2.73	2.67
Avg		2.31	3.84	3.40	2.81	

Table 1: Delta accuracy with $R = 0.4$ on the test data. A lower value denotes better performance. We **bold** the best score and underline the second-best score.

Model	CM Only		Two-Step		Joint	
	Orig	CM	Orig	CM	Orig	CM
			EmoT			
IB$_B$	45.13	66.53	69.85	68.31	74.68	67.27
IB$_L$	63.29	68.58	73.06	69.46	75.90	68.01
mB$_B$	32.97	58.11	54.72	59.68	62.98	56.54
XR$_B$	57.59	68.40	72.17	69.11	74.38	67.26
XR$_L$	**71.61**	**71.56**	**77.13**	**70.44**	**78.31**	**70.06**
			SmSA			
IB$_B$	45.10	93.51	89.81	92.68	92.52	90.71
IB$_L$	**68.40**	94.67	**90.60**	94.12	94.73	93.00
mB$_B$	51.72	83.73	78.95	85.16	85.61	84.31
XR$_B$	59.31	91.37	68.08	93.87	93.77	92.21
XR$_L$	63.06	**95.07**	85.96	**95.35**	**95.35**	**93.99**

Table 2: Accuracy on original (Orig.) and code-mixing (CM) test sets after adversarial training with different tuning strategies.

`Shot` generates $\mathcal{D}'$ from $\mathcal{D}$ and θ by utilizing the code-mixed sample generation method $g(\theta, X, Y)$. Three different fine-tuning scenarios are explored in `IndoRobusta-Shot` , i.e., **code-mixed-only tuning**, which fine-tune the model only on $\mathcal{D}'$; **two-step tuning**, which first fine-tune the model on $\mathcal{D}$, followed by a second-phase fine-tuning on $\mathcal{D}'$; and **joint training**, which fine-tunes the model on a combined dataset from $\mathcal{D}$ and $\mathcal{D}'$.

3 Experiment Setting

3.1 Dataset

We employ two Indonesian multi-class classification datasets for conducting our experiments, i.e., a sentiment-analysis dataset, SmSA (Purwarianti and Crisdayanti, 2019), and an emotion classification dataset, EmoT (Saputri et al., 2018). SmSA is a sentence-level sentiment analysis dataset consists of 12,760 samples and is labelled intro three possible sentiments values, i.e., positive, negative, and neutral. EmoT is an emotion classification dataset which consists of 4,403 samples and covers five different emotion labels, i.e., anger, fear, happiness, love, and sadness. The statistics of SmSA and EmoT datasets are shown in Appendix Table 4.

3.2 Code-mixed Sample Generation

For our experiment, we use Indonesian as the L1 language and explore four commonly used L2 languages, i.e., English, Sundanese, Javanese, and Malay. We experiment with different code-mixed perturbation ratio $R = \{0.2, 0.4, 0.6, 0.8\}$ to assess the susceptibility of models. We utilize Google Translate to translate important words to generate the code-mixed sentence X'.

3.3 Baseline Models

We include both monolingual and multilingual pre-trained LMs with various model size in our experiment. For Indonesian monolingual pre-trained LMs, we utilize two models: IndoBERT$_{\text{BASE}}$ (IB$_B$) and IndoBERT$_{\text{LARGE}}$ (IB$_L$) (Wilie et al., 2020), while for the multilingual LMs, we employ mBERT$_{\text{BASE}}$ (mB$_B$) (Devlin et al., 2019), XLM-R$_{\text{BASE}}$ (XR$_B$), and XLM-R$_{\text{LARGE}}$ (IB$_L$) (Conneau et al., 2020). Note that all of the multilingual models are knowledgeable of the Indonesian language and all L2 languages used since all the languages are covered in their pre-training corpus.

3.4 Training Setup

To evaluate the model robustness, We fine-tune the model on D using the Adam optimizer (Kingma and Ba, 2014) with a learning rate of 3e-6, and a batch size of 32. We train the model for a fixed number of epoch, i.e., 5 epochs for sentiment analysis and 10 epochs for emotion classification. We run each experiment three times using different random seeds and report the averaged score over three runs. For the adversarial training, we train the model using Adam optimizer with a learning rate of 3e-6 and a batch size of 32. We set the maximum epoch to 15, and apply early stopping with the early stopping patience set to 5.

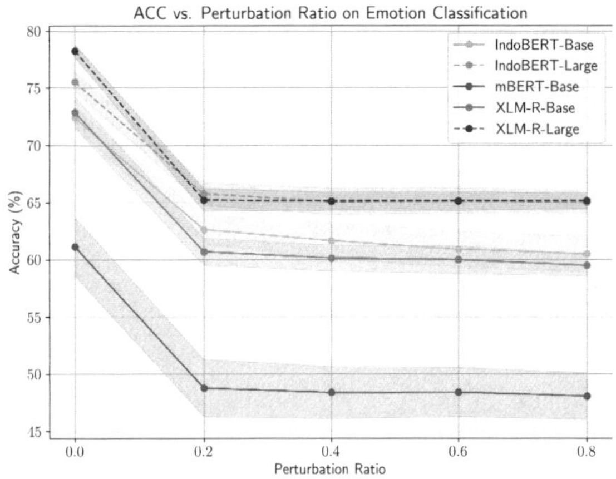

Figure 1: The effect of perturbation ratio to the evaluation accuracy in the emotion classification task.

3.5 Evaluation Setup

To measure the robustness of the models, `IndoRobusta` uses three evaluation metrics: 1) the accuracy on the monolingual dataset, 2) the accuracy on the code-mixed dataset, and 3) delta accuracy (Srinivasan et al., 2018). We measure accuracy before and after adversarial training to analyze the effectiveness of the adversarial training method in the `IndoRobusta-Shot`.

4 Result and Discussion

4.1 Code-Mixing Robustness

The result of the robustness evaluation with $R = 0.4$ is shown in Table 1. Existing LMs are more prone to code-mixing in the emotion classification task, with $> 10\%$ performance reduction, compared to 3% on the sentiment analysis task. Interestingly, monolingual models, i.e., $\text{IndoBERT}_{\text{BASE}}$ and $\text{IndoBERT}_{\text{LARGE}}$, are more robust in the emotion classification task compared to the multilingual models with 2% higher delta accuracy. While on the sentiment analysis task, all models perform almost equally good in all L2 languages.

We also observe that the robustness on English language are generally lower than Javanese and Malay in all models. We conjecture that this is due to the bias from the pre-training corpus, since pre-training corpus is gathered from online platforms, and Indonesian-English code-mixing is particularly common in such platforms (Nuraeni et al., 2018; Aulia and Laksman-Huntley, 2017; Marzona, 2017). While Indonesian and local language code-mixing are considered a secondary choice in online platforms (Cahyani et al., 2020) and is more commonly used in the day-to-day conversation (Ginting, 2019; Muslimin, 2020).

4.2 Impact of Perturbation Ratio

According to Figure 1, we can clearly observe that LMs performance gets lower as the perturbation ratio R increases. Interestingly, the steepest decline happens when the perturbation ratio $R = 0.4$, and the model performance decreases slightly with a higher perturbation ratio ($R = \{0.4, 0.6, 0.8\}$). This result suggests that translating the words with high importance as mentioned in §2.2, effectively alters the model prediction.

We further analyzed the generated code-mixed sentence, we show the example of the generated code-mixed sentences from `IndoRobusta` in Table 3. To generate the code-mixed sentence, we select important words from the sentence and perform word-level translation into four different L2 languages, i.e English, Sundanese, Javanese, and Malay. We analyze the important word selected by the I_{w_i} over a dataset, we count the total number of times a word is selected as important with $R = \{0.2, 0.4, 0.6, 0.8\}$, denoted as informative frequency (IF). For each word, we divide the IF with its document frequency (DF) to produce a normalized informative frequency (IF/DF). We show the top-20 words with highest IF/DF score for emotion classification task in Table 5 and for sentiment analysis task in Table 6. Most of the words are related to the label in the lexical-sense, e.g.: 'regret', 'disappointing', and 'disappointed' are commonly associated with **negative** sentiment, while 'comfortable', 'fun', 'nice' are commonly associated with **positive** sentiment. Most of the time, the word-translations for all L2 languages are valid and infer similar meaning. We find that the model prediction is still largely shifted even though the important word is translated correctly. This shows that, despite having learned all the languages individually, LMs are unable to generalize well on code-mixed sentences and improving robustness with an explicit tuning is required to achieve comparable performance.

4.3 Improving Code-Mixing Robustness

Table 2 shows the results of the adversarial training using different tuning strategies. **Code-mixing only** and **two-step**-tuning yield a better improvement on the code-mixed data compared to the **joint training**. Nevertheless, **code-mixing only**-tuning significantly hurts the performance on the original

Code-Mixed Text	Translation
sate kambing dan gulai kambing nya **sedap** penyajian makannan nya juga sangat cepat tempat nya cukup bersih	lamb satay and lamb curry are **yummy**, quick serving, and the place is quite clean
hayam goreng, tempe, tahu goreng dengan sambal yang pedas mantap sejak zaman dulu teu dan terjangkau	fried **chicken**, tempe, fried tofu with spicy chilli sauce has been **delicious** since ancient times.
tidak bisa **mudhun** galau mikirin lo	I cannot **sleep** because I am thinking about you
meski masa kampanye sudah selesai bukan berati habis pula **effort** mengerek tingkat kedipilihan elektabilitas.	Even though the campaign period is over, it doesn't mean that the **effort** to raise the electability level is over.

Table 3: Example of generated code-mixed sentences with `IndoRobusta`. **Blue** denotes an Malay word, Orange denotes a Sundanese word, **Red** denotes a Javanese word and **Violet** denotes an English word. The **bold words** in the translation column are the corresponding colored word translations in English.

data, while the **two-step**-tuning can retain much better performance on the original data. **joint training**, on the other hand, yields the highest performance on the original data, and even outperforms the model trained only on the original data by $\sim 2\%$ accuracy while maintaining considerably high performance on the code-mixing data.

5 Related Work

Code-Mixing in NLP Code-mixing has been studied in various language pairs such as Chinese-English (Lyu et al., 2010; Winata et al., 2019b; Lin et al., 2021; Lovenia et al., 2022), Cantonese-English (Dai et al., 2022), Hindi-English (Banerjee et al., 2018; Khanuja et al., 2020), Spanish-English (Aguilar et al., 2018; Winata et al., 2019a; Aguilar et al., 2020), Indonesian-English (Barik et al., 2019; Stymne et al., 2020), Arabic-English (Hamed et al., 2019), etc. Multiple methods have been proposed to better understand code-mixing including multi-task learning (Song et al., 2017; Winata et al., 2018), data augmentation (Winata et al., 2019b; Chang et al., 2019; Lee et al., 2019; Qin et al., 2020; Jayanthi et al., 2021; Rizvi et al., 2021), meta-learning (Winata et al., 2020), and multilingual adaptation (Winata et al., 2021). In this work, we explore code-mixing in Indonesian with four commonly used L2 languages.

Model Robustness in NLP Prior works in robustness evaluation focus on data perturbation methods (Tan and Joty, 2021; Ishii et al., 2022). Various textual perturbation methods have been introduced (Jin et al., 2019; Dhole et al., 2021), which is an essential part of robustness evaluation. Moreover, numerous efforts in improving robustness have also been explored, including adversarial training on augmented data (Li et al., 2021; Li and Specia, 2019), harmful instance removal (Bang et al., 2021; Kobayashi et al., 2020) and robust loss function (Bang et al., 2021; Zhang and Sabuncu, 2018). In this work, we focus on adversarial training, since the method is effective for handling low-resource data, such as code-mixing.

6 Conclusion

We introduce `IndoRobusta`, a framework to effectively evaluate and improve model robustness. Our results suggest adversarial training can significantly improve the code-mixing robustness of LMs, while at the same time, improving the performance on the monolingual data. Moreover, we show that existing LMs are more robust to English code-mixed and conjecture that this comes from the source bias in the existing pre-training corpora.

Limitations

One of the limitation of our approach is that we utilize Google Translate to generate the perturbed code-mixing samples instead of manually generating natural code-mixing sentences. Common mistake made from the generated code-mixed sentence is on translating ambiguous terms, which produces inaccurate word-level translation and alters the meaning of the sentence. For future work, we expect to build a higher quality code-mixed sentences to better assess the code-mixed robustness of the existing Indonesian large-pretrained language models.

Acknowledgements

We sincerely thank the anonymous reviewers for their insightful comments on our paper.

References

Gustavo Aguilar, Fahad AlGhamdi, Victor Soto, Mona Diab, Julia Hirschberg, and Thamar Solorio. 2018. Overview of the CALCS 2018 Shared Task: named entity recognition on code-switched data. In *Proceedings of the Third Workshop on Computational Approaches to Linguistic Code-Switching*, Melbourne, Australia. Association for Computational Linguistics.

Gustavo Aguilar, Sudipta Kar, and Thamar Solorio. 2020. Lince: A centralized benchmark for linguistic code-switching evaluation. In *Proceedings of the 12th Language Resources and Evaluation Conference*, pages 1803–1813.

Alham Aji, Genta Indra Winata, Fajri Koto, Samuel Cahyawijaya, Ade Romadhony, Rahmad Mahendra, Kemal Kurniawan, David Moeljadi, Radityo Eko Prasojo, Timothy Baldwin, et al. 2022. One country, 700+ languages: Nlp challenges for underrepresented languages and dialects in indonesia. In *Proceedings of the 60th Annual Meeting of the Association for Computational Linguistics (Volume 1: Long Papers)*, pages 7226–7249.

M. Aulia and M. Laksman-Huntley. 2017. Indonesian-english code-switching on social media. In *Cultural Dynamics in a Globalized World*, pages 791–796. Routledge.

Suman Banerjee, Nikita Moghe, Siddhartha Arora, and Mitesh M. Khapra. 2018. A dataset for building code-mixed goal oriented conversation systems. In *Proceedings of the 27th International Conference on Computational Linguistics*, pages 3766–3780, Santa Fe, New Mexico, USA. Association for Computational Linguistics.

Yejin Bang, Etsuko Ishii, Samuel Cahyawijaya, Ziwei Ji, and Pascale Fung. 2021. Model generalization on covid-19 fake news detection. In *CONSTRAINT@AAAI*.

Anab Maulana Barik, Rahmad Mahendra, and Mirna Adriani. 2019. Normalization of indonesian-english code-mixed twitter data. In *Proceedings of the 5th Workshop on Noisy User-generated Text (W-NUT 2019)*, pages 417–424.

Hilda Cahyani, Umi Tursini, and Nurenzia Yannuar. 2020. Mixing and switching in social media: Denoting the indonesian "keminggris" language. 10:2020.

Samuel Cahyawijaya, Genta Indra Winata, Bryan Wilie, Karissa Vincentio, Xiaohong Li, Adhiguna Kuncoro, Sebastian Ruder, Zhi Yuan Lim, Syafri Bahar, Masayu Leylia Khodra, Ayu Purwarianti, and Pascale Fung. 2021. Indonlg: Benchmark and resources for evaluating indonesian natural language generation.

Ching-Ting Chang, Shun-Po Chuang, and Hung-Yi Lee. 2019. Code-switching sentence generation by generative adversarial networks and its application to data augmentation. *Proc. Interspeech 2019*, pages 554–558.

Alexis Conneau, Kartikay Khandelwal, Naman Goyal, Vishrav Chaudhary, Guillaume Wenzek, Francisco Guzmán, Edouard Grave, Myle Ott, Luke Zettlemoyer, and Veselin Stoyanov. 2020. Unsupervised cross-lingual representation learning at scale. In *Proceedings of the 58th Annual Meeting of the Association for Computational Linguistics*, pages 8440–8451, Online. Association for Computational Linguistics.

Wenliang Dai, Samuel Cahyawijaya, Tiezheng Yu, Elham J. Barezi, Peng Xu, Cheuk Tung YIU, Rita Frieske, Holy Lovenia, Genta Winata, Qifeng Chen, Xiaojuan Ma, Bertram Shi, and Pascale Fung. 2022. Ci-avsr: A cantonese audio-visual speech datasetfor in-car command recognition. In *Proceedings of the Language Resources and Evaluation Conference*, pages 6786–6793, Marseille, France. European Language Resources Association.

Jacob Devlin, Ming-Wei Chang, Kenton Lee, and Kristina Toutanova. 2019. BERT: Pre-training of deep bidirectional transformers for language understanding. In *Proceedings of the 2019 Conference of the North American Chapter of the Association for Computational Linguistics: Human Language Technologies, Volume 1 (Long and Short Papers)*, pages 4171–4186, Minneapolis, Minnesota. Association for Computational Linguistics.

Nindian Puspa Dewi, Joan Santoso, Ubaidi Ubaidi, and Eka Rahayu Setyaningsih. 2020. Combination of genetic algorithm and brill tagger algorithm for part of speech tagging bahasa madura. *Proceeding of the Electrical Engineering Computer Science and Informatics*, 7(0).

Kaustubh D Dhole, Varun Gangal, Sebastian Gehrmann, Aadesh Gupta, Zhenhao Li, Saad Mahamood, Abinaya Mahendiran, Simon Mille, Ashish Srivastava, Samson Tan, et al. 2021. Nl-augmenter: A framework for task-sensitive natural language augmentation. *arXiv preprint arXiv:2112.02721*.

Carolin Rninta Ginting. 2019. Analysis of code-switching and code-mixing in the learning process of indonesia subject at grade 3 of SD negeri 2 jayagiri. In *Proceedings of the Eleventh Conference on Applied Linguistics (CONAPLIN 2018)*. Atlantis Press.

Injy Hamed, Moritz Zhu, Mohamed Elmahdy, Slim Abdennadher, and Ngoc Thang Vu. 2019. Code-switching language modeling with bilingual word embeddings: A case study for egyptian arabic-english. In *International Conference on Speech and Computer*, pages 160–170. Springer.

Etsuko Ishii, Yan Xu, Samuel Cahyawijaya, and Bryan Wilie. 2022. Can question rewriting help conversational question answering? In *Proceedings of the Third Workshop on Insights from Negative Results in NLP*, pages 94–99, Dublin, Ireland. Association for Computational Linguistics.

Sai Muralidhar Jayanthi, Kavya Nerella, Khyathi Raghavi Chandu, and Alan W Black. 2021. Codemixednlp: An extensible and open nlp toolkit for code-mixing. In *Proceedings of the Fifth Workshop on Computational Approaches to Linguistic Code-Switching*, pages 113–118.

Di Jin, Zhijing Jin, Joey Tianyi Zhou, and Peter Szolovits. 2019. Is bert really robust? a strong baseline for natural language attack on text classification and entailment.

Muhammad Fiqri Khaikal and Arie Ardiyanti Suryani. 2021. Statistical machine translation dayak language – indonesia language. *Informatika Mulawarman : Jurnal Ilmiah Ilmu Komputer*, 16(1):49.

Simran Khanuja, Sandipan Dandapat, Anirudh Srinivasan, Sunayana Sitaram, and Monojit Choudhury. 2020. Gluecos: An evaluation benchmark for code-switched nlp. In *Proceedings of the 58th Annual Meeting of the Association for Computational Linguistics*, pages 3575–3585.

Diederik P Kingma and Jimmy Ba. 2014. Adam: A method for stochastic optimization. *arXiv preprint arXiv:1412.6980*.

Sosuke Kobayashi, Sho Yokoi, Jun Suzuki, and Kentaro Inui. 2020. Efficient estimation of influence of a training instance. In *Proceedings of SustaiNLP: Workshop on Simple and Efficient Natural Language Processing*, pages 41–47, Online. Association for Computational Linguistics.

Fajri Koto, Afshin Rahimi, Jey Han Lau, and Timothy Baldwin. 2020. Indolem and indobert: A benchmark dataset and pre-trained language model for indonesian nlp.

Grandee Lee, Xianghu Yue, and Haizhou Li. 2019. Linguistically motivated parallel data augmentation for code-switch language modeling. In *Interspeech*, pages 3730–3734.

Zhenhao Li and Lucia Specia. 2019. Improving neural machine translation robustness via data augmentation: Beyond back-translation. In *Proceedings of the 5th Workshop on Noisy User-generated Text (W-NUT 2019)*, pages 328–336, Hong Kong, China. Association for Computational Linguistics.

Zongyi Li, Jianhan Xu, Jiehang Zeng, Linyang Li, Xiaoqing Zheng, Qi Zhang, Kai-Wei Chang, and Cho-Jui Hsieh. 2021. Searching for an effective defender: Benchmarking defense against adversarial word substitution.

Zhaojiang Lin, Andrea Madotto, Genta Indra Winata, Peng Xu, Feijun Jiang, Yuxiang Hu, Chen Shi, and Pascale Fung. 2021. Bitod: A bilingual multi-domain dataset for task-oriented dialogue modeling. In *Thirty-fifth Conference on Neural Information Processing Systems Datasets and Benchmarks Track (Round 1)*.

Holy Lovenia, Samuel Cahyawijaya, Genta Winata, Peng Xu, Yan Xu, Zihan Liu, Rita Frieske, Tiezheng Yu, Wenliang Dai, Elham J. Barezi, Qifeng Chen, Xiaojuan Ma, Bertram Shi, and Pascale Fung. 2022. Ascend: A spontaneous chinese-english dataset for code-switching in multi-turn conversation. In *Proceedings of the Language Resources and Evaluation Conference*, pages 7259–7268, Marseille, France. European Language Resources Association.

Dau-Cheng Lyu, Tien Ping Tan, Chng Eng Siong, and Haizhou Li. 2010. Seame: a mandarin-english code-switching speech corpus in south-east asia. In *INTERSPEECH*.

Yessy Marzona. 2017. The use of code mixing between indonesian and english in indonesian advertisement of gadis.

Afif Ikhwanul Muslimin. 2020. Code-mixing of javanese language and bahasa indonesia in the friday prayer sermon at miftahul hidayah mosque, pendem village, city of batu, east java. *MABASAN*, 14(2):277–296.

Carol Myers-Scotton and Janice Jake. 2009. A universal model of code-switching and bilingual language processing and production. *The Cambridge Handbook of Linguistic Code-switching*, pages 336–357.

Bani Nuraeni, Mochammad Farid, and Sri Cahyati. 2018. The use of indonesian english code mixing on instagram captions. *PROJECT (Professional Journal of English Education)*, 1:448.

Ayu Purwarianti and Ida Ayu Putu Ari Crisdayanti. 2019. Improving bi-lstm performance for indonesian sentiment analysis using paragraph vector. In *2019 International Conference of Advanced Informatics: Concepts, Theory and Applications (ICAICTA)*, pages 1–5. IEEE.

Libo Qin, Minheng Ni, Yue Zhang, and Wanxiang Che. 2020. Cosda-ml: Multi-lingual code-switching data augmentation for zero-shot cross-lingual nlp. *ArXiv*, abs/2006.06402.

Mohd Sanad Zaki Rizvi, Anirudh Srinivasan, Tanuja Ganu, Monojit Choudhury, and Sunayana Sitaram. 2021. Gcm: A toolkit for generating synthetic code-mixed text. In *Proceedings of the 16th Conference of the European Chapter of the Association for Computational Linguistics: System Demonstrations*, pages 205–211.

Mei Silviana Saputri, Rahmad Mahendra, and Mirna Adriani. 2018. Emotion classification on indonesian twitter dataset. In *2018 International Conference on Asian Language Processing (IALP)*, pages 90–95. IEEE.

Xiao Song, Yuexian Zou, Shilei Huang, Shaobin Chen, and Yi Liu. 2017. Investigating multi-task learning for automatic speech recognition with code-switching between mandarin and english. In *2017 International Conference on Asian Language Processing (IALP)*, pages 27–30.

Vignesh Srinivasan, Arturo Marban, Klaus-Robert Müller, Wojciech Samek, and Shinichi Nakajima. 2018. Robustifying models against adversarial attacks by langevin dynamics.

Sara Stymne et al. 2020. Evaluating word embeddings for indonesian–english code-mixed text based on synthetic data. In *Proceedings of the The 4th Workshop on Computational Approaches to Code Switching*, pages 26–35.

Samson Tan and Shafiq Joty. 2021. Code-mixing on sesame street: Dawn of the adversarial polyglots. In *Proceedings of the 2021 Conference of the North American Chapter of the Association for Computational Linguistics: Human Language Technologies*, pages 3596–3616.

Novi Safriadi Tri Apriani, Herry Sujaini. 2016. Pengaruh kuantitas korpus terhadap akurasi mesin penerjemah statistik bahasa bugis wajo ke bahasa indonesia. *Jurnal Sistem dan Teknologi Informasi*, 4(1):168–173.

Bryan Wilie, Karissa Vincentio, Genta Indra Winata, Samuel Cahyawijaya, Xiaohong Li, Zhi Yuan Lim, Sidik Soleman, Rahmad Mahendra, Pascale Fung, Syafri Bahar, and Ayu Purwarianti. 2020. Indonlu: Benchmark and resources for evaluating indonesian natural language understanding.

Genta Indra Winata, Alham Fikri Aji, Samuel Cahyawijaya, Rahmad Mahendra, Fajri Koto, Ade Romadhony, Kemal Kurniawan, David Moeljadi, Radityo Eko Prasojo, Pascale Fung, Timothy Baldwin, Jey Han Lau, Rico Sennrich, and Sebastian Ruder. 2022. Nusax: Multilingual parallel sentiment dataset for 10 indonesian local languages.

Genta Indra Winata, Samuel Cahyawijaya, Zhaojiang Lin, Zihan Liu, Peng Xu, and Pascale Fung. 2020. Meta-transfer learning for code-switched speech recognition. In *Proceedings of the 58th Annual Meeting of the Association for Computational Linguistics*, pages 3770–3776, Online. Association for Computational Linguistics.

Genta Indra Winata, Samuel Cahyawijaya, Zihan Liu, Zhaojiang Lin, Andrea Madotto, and Pascale Fung. 2021. Are multilingual models effective in code-switching? In *Proceedings of the Fifth Workshop on Computational Approaches to Linguistic Code-Switching*, pages 142–153, Online. Association for Computational Linguistics.

Genta Indra Winata, Zhaojiang Lin, and Pascale Ngan Fung. 2019a. Learning multilingual meta-embeddings for code-switching named entity recognition. In *Proceedings of the 4th Workshop on Representation Learning for NLP (RepL4NLP-2019)*.

Genta Indra Winata, Andrea Madotto, Chien-Sheng Wu, and Pascale Fung. 2018. Code-switching language modeling using syntax-aware multi-task learning. In *Proceedings of the Third Workshop on Computational Approaches to Linguistic Code-Switching*, pages 62–67, Melbourne, Australia. Association for Computational Linguistics.

Genta Indra Winata, Andrea Madotto, Chien-Sheng Wu, and Pascale Fung. 2019b. Code-switched language models using neural based synthetic data from parallel sentences. In *Proceedings of the 23rd Conference on Computational Natural Language Learning (CoNLL)*, pages 271–280, Hong Kong, China. Association for Computational Linguistics.

Zhilu Zhang and Mert R. Sabuncu. 2018. Generalized cross entropy loss for training deep neural networks with noisy labels. In *Proceedings of the 32nd International Conference on Neural Information Processing Systems*, NIPS'18, page 87928802, Red Hook, NY, USA. Curran Associates Inc.

A Annotation Guideline for Human Evaluation

We introduce a manual annotation to evaluate the generated code-mixed sentences. To validate the quality of our perturbed code-mixing sentences, we hire 3 native annotators for each language to evaluate the generated Sundanese-Indonesian and Javanese-Indonesian code-mixed sentences, and 3 Indonesian annotators with professional English proficiency for assessing the generated English-Indonesian code-mixed sentences. Each human annotator is asked to assess the quality of 40 randomly sampled code-mixed sentences and provide a score in range of $[1, 2, 3, 4, 5]$ with 1 denotes an incomprehensible code-mixing sentence and 5 denotes a perfectly natural code-mixed sentence. The detailed annotation guideline is described in A The score between annotators are averaged to reduce annotation bias.

Dataset	|Train|	|Valid|	|Test|	#Class
EmoT	3,521	440	442	5
SmSA	11,000	1,260	500	3

Table 4: Statistics of EmoT and SmSA datasets.

Table 4 contains more details of the EmoT and SmSA dataset that we used in the sample generation. Sample generated by perturbing these datasets will later be annotated.

First, we compile 40 samples generated from each model into an excel sheet. Then the annotator is given access to the file. Before starting the annotation process, the annotator is given instructions and a definition of the score that can be assigned to the sample sentence. For each row in the given excel file, the annotator is asked to read the code-mixing sentence generated by the model and provide annotation values. Annotation scores are defined as follows:

1 - unnatural (unintelligible sentence)

2 - less natural (sentences can be understood even though they are strange)

3 - adequately natural (sentences can be understood even though they are not used correctly)

4 - imperfect natural (sentences are easy to understand, but some of the words used are slightly inaccurate)

5 - natural (sentences are easy to understand and appropriate to use)

B Annotation Result

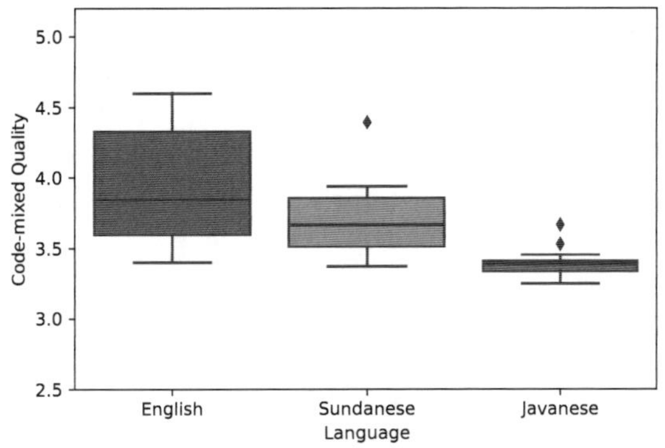

Figure 2: Human evaluation result from the generated code-mixed samples averaged over three annotators.

Figure 2 shows the result of the human assessment on the generated code-mixed sentences. The results indicates that the generated sentences are adequately natural by achieving an average score of 3.94 for English-Indonesian, 3.71 for Sundanese-Indonesian, and 3.39 for Javanese-Indonesian.

Word	IF	DF	IF/DF	jw	ms	su	en
love	1078	1260	0.856	tresna	cinta	cinta	love
tolong	1408	2520	0.559	bantuan	membantu	Tulung	help
km	1183	2520	0.469	km	km	km	km
kasih	2947	6300	0.468	tresna	cinta	cinta	love
pakai	1505	3360	0.448	nggunakake	guna	ngagunakeun	use
udh	1659	3780	0.439	wis	Sudah	Geus	Already
setan	1088	2520	0.432	setan	syaitan	Sétan	Devil
hrs	1078	2520	0.428	**jam**	**jam**	**tabuh**	**hrs**
cinta	5559	13020	0.427	tresna	cinta	**cinta**	love
jam	2495	5880	0.424	jam	pukul	tabuh	o'clock
gua	1594	3780	0.422	aku	saya	abdi	I
jatuh	1768	4200	0.421	tiba	jatuh	ragrag ka handap	fall down
mobil	1057	2520	0.419	mobil	kereta	mobil	car
sehat	1214	2940	0.413	**sehat**	sihat	cageur	healthy
beneran	1351	3360	0.402	tenan	sungguh	saleresna	really
kadang	1175	2940	0.400	kadhangkala	kadang-kadang	sakapeung	sometimes
lu	1505	3780	0.398	**lu**	**lu**	**lu**	**lu**
ketemu	1641	4200	0.391	ketemu	berjumpa	papanggih	meet
dgn	2254	5880	0.383	karo	dengan	kalawan	with
kantor	1127	2940	0.383	kantor	pejabat	kantor	office

Table 5: Top 20 most perturbed word on **emotion classification** experiments conducted on test data and their translation on four languages. **Red** denotes mistranslated words due to ambiguity or translator limitation.

Word	IF	DF	IF/DF	jw	ms	su	en
cocok	1750	2100	0.833	cocok	sesuai	cocog	suitable
asik	2338	2940	0.795	Asik	Asik	Asik	Asik
nyaman	2905	3780	0.769	nyaman	selesa	sreg	comfortable
menyesal	2240	2940	0.76	getun	penyesalan	kaduhung	regret
mantap	8456	11340	0.746	ajeg	mantap	ajeg	steady
mengecewakan	3094	4200	0.737	nguciwani	mengecewakan	nguciwakeun	disappointing
kecewa	21910	30660	0.715	kuciwa	kecewa	kuciwa	disappointed
enak	9443	14700	0.642	**becik**	bagus	hade	nice
jelek	1617	2520	0.642	ala	teruk	goréng	bad
salut	1834	2940	0.624	salam	tabik hormat	salam	salute
memuaskan	2877	4620	0.623	marem	memuaskan	nyugemakeun	satisfying
keren	3136	5040	0.622	**kelangan**	**sejuk**	tiis	cool
kadaluarsa	1827	2940	0.621	kadaluarsa	tamat tempoh	kadaluwarsa	expired
murah	3094	5040	0.614	murah	murah	murah	inexpensive
kartu	2058	3360	0.613	kertu	kad	kartu	card
banget	2434	41160	0.591	banget	sangat	pisan	very
bangga	148	2520	0.589	bangga	bangga	reueus	proud
mending	1974	3360	0.588	luwih apik	lebih baik	Leuwih alus	Better
uang	4396	7560	0.581	dhuwit	wang	duit	money
id	1442	2520	0.572	id	ID	**en**	id

Table 6: Top 20 most perturbed word on **sentiment analysis** experiments conducted on test data and their translation on four languages. **Red** denotes mistranslated words due to ambiguity or translator limitation.

Author Index

Association for Computational Linguistics
209 N. Eighth Street
Stroudsburg, Pennsylvania 18360

ISBN 978-1-7138-6318-2

CURRAN ASSOCIATES INC.
proceedings.com

Sixth Workshop on Universal Dependencies (UDW 2023)

Washington, DC, USA
9-12 March 2023